Xmas 2021

I have enjoy
of us den
leganding SP

Love,
Joe; Ion

AN A – Z OF
CHRISTIAN TRUTH
AND EXPERIENCE

AN A – Z OF CHRISTIAN TRUTH AND EXPERIENCE

*Drawn from Some of the Leading
Writers of the Christian Centuries*

J. GRAHAM MILLER

THE BANNER OF TRUTH TRUST

THE BANNER OF TRUTH TRUST
3 Murrayfield Road, Edinburgh EH12 6EL, UK
P O Box 621, Carlisle, PA 17013, USA

*

© J. Graham Miller 2003
ISBN 0 85151 836 2

*

Typeset in 11 / 12 pt Perpetua at
the Banner of Truth Trust
Printed in Great Britain by
Scotprint, Haddington,
Scotland

Contents

Introduction

The day I was welcomed to the home of Graham and Flora Miller was a milestone in my life and the beginning of a treasured friendship. The place was the manse of St Giles Presbyterian Church, in the Sydney suburb of Hurstville, and the year 1979. It was the concluding year of Dr Miller's ministry, and he and Flora were shortly to move south to the home purchased for retirement years in the country town of Wangaratta, Victoria. After that date we were to be frequently in touch, but it was not until a visit to Wangaratta in 1999 that I discovered something which filled me with interest and led to the present book. Before I explain, something more needs to be said on why these two friends have meant so much to so many.

The strong Presbyterian churches of New Zealand of the nineteenth century were established by an immigrant stock that had known a revived evangelicalism in Scotland. Among that number were the parents of Thomas Miller, then an infant, who arrived in Dunedin in 1878. In due course Thomas Miller graduated with honours at the University of Otago and, with his heart set on the gospel ministry, received his training at the Theological Hall in Dunedin. Married to a fellow-Scot, Marion Strang, their lives were to be given to successive parishes in the

Presbyterian Church of New Zealand, concluding at St Stephen's, Dunedin. The years of Mr Miller's ministry coincided with the time in the Church when early promise in the pulpits had given way to liberalism. A minority stood firm and, by his faithful preaching and his evangelistic work among young men, Thomas Miller was at their centre. For this leadership there was a price to pay. Commenting on it, the Rev. Neil Macleod has written: 'Despite bitter criticism, and derisory notes, Thomas Miller remained a loving, loyal beacon-light to the waverers and the timid ones within his own Presbyterian Church and far beyond.'[1]

It was while the Millers were still serving at Rangiora, Canterbury, that John Graham, the second of their seven children and the eldest son, was born on 8 October 1913. Educated at Palmerston North and Otago Boys High Schools, he proceeded to a law office in Dunedin, and, studying law part-time, graduated LL.B. from the University of New Zealand. By that time he was already a committed Christian, as he writes in the Foreword which follows this Introduction. Like Calvin before him, Graham – as he is known to his friends – proceeded from law to the Christian ministry, entering his denomination's Theological Hall, Knox College, in 1939. This decision cannot have been altogether easy, for, as he writes:

> As father's eldest son I was early made aware of his situation in the Presbyterian Church of New Zealand, then the most influential denomination in the country. Liberalism ruled with grave composure in the courts of the Church and evangelicals were a tolerated and influential minority.

[1] Foreword to *Evangelism and the Reformed Faith, and Other Essays Commemorating the Ministry of J. Graham Miller*, ed. C. R. Thomas (Sydney: Presbyterian Church of Australia, 1980).   [2] Personal letter to the writer, 8 May 2000.

A – Z OF CHRISTIAN TRUTH AND EXPERIENCE

Father was one of a few ministers who maintained a digni-
fied and often lonely position in the courts of the Church.
He was a member of the Theological Education Committee
and the College was only a mile from his church (St
Stephen's) on the fringe of his parish. As President of the
Evangelical Bible League of Otago father wrote *Archaeology
and the Bible* in 1934. I was then president of the Evangelical Union of Otago University. Its formation had been
opposed in the governing Student Union because of SCM
pressure, but its registration as a student body was
approved on the influence of the student President of the
university. When I entered Knox College as a student for
the ministry in 1939 several Evangelical Union men were
in the College. We met weekly for prayer in the study of
one of these men, an action which was resented by some
men as divisive. By the end of term one of 1939 I came to
the realisation that all three professors has laid a plan to
unsettle new students who retained faith in the historic
inerrancy of the Scriptures.'[2]

Student days at Knox College were brightened by his court-
ship with Flora McDonald from Southland. They were married
in 1941 and, answering a call to a mission field in which New
Zealand Christians had long been interested, sailed together for
the New Hebrides (now Vanuatu). It was the eve of one of the
darkest periods in World War II when no one knew how far the
Japanese advance into the southern Pacific would extend.
Graham Miller served in the Australian Navy's boat-watching
organization until United States troops took over the
responsibility in mid-1942. The Millers' island base was Tongoa
from 1941 to April 1947, when Graham became Principal of
the Missions Training Institute for pastors and teachers, on the
islet of Tangoa. There in 1948 the Presbyterian Church of the

New Hebrides (now Vanuatu) was constituted with Graham Miller as its first moderator.

The Millers moved from the New Hebrides in 1953, but the bond with the church was to be permanent, and when that Assembly established a Bible College at Tangoa in 1971 it was their friend they called back to be its first Principal. The call was accepted, and so followed a second period in the New Hebrides until 1973. Thereafter there were to be a number of visits (the last in August 1998 on the occasion of the Golden Jubilee of the church). Out of these missionary years came his major literary work, *Live: A History of Church Planting in the New Hebrides*. The main title was taken from the sentence in Ezekiel 16:6, 'I said unto thee . . . Live.' This definitive and often thrilling work, written for the people of Vanuatu, was published in seven separate books, the first in 1978 and the last in 1990. The first carried a dedication in a poem they had both written which began,

> Islands of the New Hebrides
> We remember
> The silver moon,
> The stormy wind,
> The soft sunset
> And the rush of rain on the forest's roof;
> The rustling fronds of the palm,
> The smell of copra,
> Seasickness,
> The scream of the siviri,
> And the sudden trembling of the earth;
> The night sky bright with wildfire,
> The graves and the gardens
> And the banyan's shade.

One of his former students on Tangoa, Dr Titus Path, has written: 'The name of J.G. Miller will live for ever in the hearts and upon the lips of myriads who have come to know the Saviour as he has shown Him by word, deed and pen.'[3]

The years between the two periods of missionary service in Vanuatu were spent serving the First Presbyterian Church of Papakura, in south Auckland, from February 1953; then, from 1966, as Principal of the Melbourne Bible Institute. The latter period saw the Institute – later the Bible College of Victoria – reach an enrolment of over 200. During these years in New Zealand and Australia there were many additional labours. Dr Miller was one of the founders and regular writers for *Evangelical Presbyterian*, the organ of the Westminster Fellowship within the Presbyterian Church of New Zealand. The magazine reached its zenith in the 1960s and among Graham Miller's contributions was an extended series of 'Studies in Hosea' (January 1964–May 1965). He was also widely sought after as a preacher and helper and was to be found in places as far afield as Keswick, in England; Berlin (the Congress on Evangelism of 1966); and India, where he undertook conferences for pastors, under the auspices of the Evangelical Fellowship of India.

From the Millers' second period in the New Hebrides they returned to Australia, this time to the congregation of St Giles, Sydney, New South Wales, in 1974. Fruitful years followed. St Giles was already numerically the strongest Presbyterian congregation in south Sydney. Under Dr Graham Miller's definite and winsome biblical ministry there was a deepening of the life of the church, and conversions which provided workers for years to come. To this day recordings of many of the sermons he preached at St Giles continue to be broadcast weekly on Sydney local radio.[4]

---

[3] Foreword to *Workbook on Christian Doctrine*, J. G. Miller (Lawson, NSW: Mission Publications of Australia, 1974).
[4] A half-hour programme on Wednesday evenings called 'The Bread of Life'.

But in the providence of God there was a vital wider work for Graham Miller to do in his years in New South Wales. The Presbyterian Church of Australia was at the most critical point of its history. For some years many in the leadership of the denomination, strongly influenced by the international ethos of ecumenism, had been pressing for a reunion among the Australian Churches, and proposals for union with Methodists and Congregationalists were already before the Presbyterian Church in 1974. The situation in New South Wales was particularly critical and Mark Hutchinson, a recent historian of the denomination, has rightly noted the significance of Graham Miller's arrival at that juncture. Having been a leader, he says, in New Zealand, he was already 'a consistent fighter against union on missiological and theological grounds'. Dr Hutchinson illustrates this by the following quotation from the *Evangelical Presbyterian*:

> The real scandal of Christendom is not the denominational differences in the Protestant Church. The real scandal of Christendom is the spiritually-bankrupt liberalism, the phoney intellectualism, the sceptical neo-orthodoxy, the outright apostasy which is corrupting the very vitals of the Church of Jesus Christ.[5]

The activity of Graham Miller and others resulted in the fact that, when union took place and the 'Uniting Church' was inaugurated on 22 June 1977, no less than fifty per cent of the New South Wales churches stayed out and continued as the Presbyterian Church.

Yet to emphasize this alone would be misleading. He is remembered chiefly in New South Wales today by the individuals

---

[5] Mark Hutchinson, *Iron In Our Blood: A History of the Presbyterian Church in NSW, 1788–2001* (Sydney: Ferguson Publications, 2001), p. 370. The author of the quotation is not given but it undoubtedly represents what Graham Miller believed.

A – Z OF CHRISTIAN TRUTH AND EXPERIENCE

he helped spiritually, and particularly by the numerous younger men whom he strengthened and guided with regard to the Christian ministry. These younger men formed the main contributors to the book, *Evangelism and the Reformed Faith, and Other Essays Commemorating the Ministry of J. Graham Miller*, published in 1980 (see footnote 1). Its editor, the Rev. C. R. Thomas, spoke for them all when he wrote of Miller in the Introduction:

> During the past five years, one of the major emphases of his ministry has been his encouragement to brother ministers, old and young, and the leading of a remarkable number of men to present themselves as candidates for the Ministry of the Word . . . Each one of us acknowledges that Graham Miller is a beloved pastor, teacher and friend, whose life and ministry have been an example and encouragement to us all.'[6]

Without these younger men the Church situation in NSW would have been far weaker in the last quarter century.[7]

This brings me back to the discovery made on the visit to Wangaratta in February 1999. It was the first sight I had of a number of well-bound volumes, filled with my friend's firm and distinctive hand-writing. They were what an older generation of ministers once called 'common-place books' – books made up of memorable quotations, gleaned and recorded from leading

---

[6] *Evangelism and the Reformed Faith*, p. ix.
[7] I cannot vouch for the accuracy of the following figures relating to the Presbyterian Church of Australia, but they are interesting. It is, 'At the time of Union in 1977 only about 40 per cent of the ministers who continued in parish ministry in Victoria and New South Wales could be described as "evangelical" . . . Today the percentage of evangelicals in parish ministry is about 80 per cent ... and most of the more than one hundred new ministers since 1977 are Calvinistic.' Rowland S. Ward, *The Bush Still Burns: The Presbyterian and Reformed Faith in Australia, 1788-1988* (Melbourne, 1989), p. 466. To say this is not to deny that there are many other problems affecting the ministry besides liberalism.

authors, and worthy of being retained. Graham Miller long followed this practice and his testimony was that by it his ministry 'ever since had been informed, sustained and illuminated by the resources patiently gathered in this way'. One of the first titles he treated in this way was Canon H. P. Liddon's Bampton Lectures on *The Divinity of Our Lord* which, at the age of twenty-one, he came across in a second-hand bookshop in Dunedin. 'I found', he recalled, 'I had in my grasp a handful of pure gold.' He uses the same analogy in speaking of his practice of collecting quotations in the Foreword which follows.

A sight of some of this 'gold' convinced me of the benefit which others could also gain from what had been the work of a life-time. The weight of the original far exceeds a single volume, but in these pages Dr Miller has kindly provided a selection and one which gives a wonderful 'overview' of the Christian faith drawn from many of the classic authors of the church. I have found the contents humbling and inspiring. They require, it should be said, pondering and reflection more than consecutive reading. John Wesley's maxim is especially applicable, 'Read a little, pray and meditate much.'

The great truths, so prominent here, have been left on the edge and in the shadows in much contemporary Christian thought. Sometimes they are not so much denied as simply left aside. If this book represents true biblical Christianity, and real Christian experience, then we have good reason to be humbled before God. A great heritage has come down to us and once again its continuance is threatened. But we need not fear, for at its heart is the Word of God that lives and abides for ever. We may say of it what Beza said to the King of Navarre concerning the church, 'May it please you to remember that it is an anvil which has worn out many hammers.'

IAIN H. MURRAY
Edinburgh, March 2003

Foreword

As the second of seven children in a Presbyterian manse in New Zealand I had no early thoughts of the Ministry. Both our parents prayed and worked quietly to bring us children to Christ. Family worship took place daily after breakfast and before we hurried off to school, and again in the early evening after tea. It began with a hymn from Sankey. Father then read from a well-worn Bible in the Authorized Version. The plan was to read through the Bible. The literature, the language, the long names, the lively episodes sank into our subconscious memories. One day, in Sunday school, one of the boys tossed a Bible across the classroom to another lad who had none. The teacher, a middle-aged farmer who brought a carload of children to Sunday school in his Model T Ford, looked reproachfully at the lad who had so demeaned the Bible. We all sensed his meaning.

Sunday school examinations were held annually for the whole denomination. Mother, an ex-teacher, prepared us for these. One section comprised portions of scripture which had to be memorized and written down from memory in the examination. Those portions of Scripture have remained with me ever since. How well-chosen they were: the Ten Commandments from Exodus 20; the Beatitudes from Matthew 5; Isaiah 53 and 55; Psalm 103; John 14; Ephesians 6 (the complete armour).

I was 14 when father called me into his study and dealt with me about my need of the Saviour. It was an unhurried session with his open Bible before my eyes and conscience. I was an awkward convert as we knelt and I repeated a prayer of confession and faith after the words spoken by my father. But, within two weeks, I recognized a change in my own life, disposition, tastes and habits. In retrospect I date my conversion from that time. I thereafter made my public profession of faith and was received into the membership of the church. Father planned annual summer holidays at the beach. This was made economical by our exchanging manses with another manse family for the month of January (Southern Hemisphere summer).

I had just turned 15. We were at a lovely South Otago holiday spot, great for fishing and rabbiting. There was only one service on the Sunday. Father took me aside and said, 'I would suggest you read Romans today.'

The next Sunday he repeated the suggestion.

On four successive Sundays I read Romans.

By the time I was 25, and a student for the ministry, I understood father's far-sighted intentions. Romans was to become the life-blood of my preaching. Now in retirement, after 60 years of harvesting the seed thoughts of others, I have gathered together extracts which bear upon Holy Scripture. In the pulpit, in the courts of the church, in the public media and in casual conversation the Bible takes its imperturbable course, delighting its lovers, confounding its critics and confronting each new generation with its freshness and indestructibility.

Gold brought the first substantial influx of migrants to Australia. One of the simplest methods of discovering gold was panning for tiny flakes in mountain streams. Over the years of reading, amidst the shingle and soil of one's reading there have turned up the flakes of shining gold. From the age of about twenty, I began to treasure these quotations in durable volumes, indexing them under appropriate themes, and it is a selection from this lifelong labour that has here been prepared for publication.

The reader will notice my debt to the Reformers, and especially to John Calvin. The Banner of Truth Trust has done a vital service in publishing Calvin's sermons in recent years. I have greatly valued the facsimile editions of the sermons on the book of Job, on Deuteronomy and on Timothy and Titus. The Elizabethan English, far from hindering my reading, gave added piquancy to Calvin's pulpit ministry.

My ministry has been informed, sustained and illuminated by the resources patiently gathered in this way, and the process of assembling the flakes of gold for publication has renewed my gratitude to God for leading me into the way of life and into the ministry of His Word.

J. GRAHAM MILLER
Victoria, Australia
March 2003

NOTES

1. In the alphabetical sequence which follows, quotations grouped together, with no individual source given, are from the author named at the end of the group.
2. The list at the end of the book gives the sources from which most of the quotations were taken, or, where the source is now uncertain, a brief notice of the author concerned.

ABILITY

When God calls us to any charge He also gives us the ability to accomplish that which He commanded.

Confidence in ourselves produces carelessness and arrogance.

God distributes His Spirit to those whom He intends to apply to His service.

JOHN CALVIN

ADAM

The transgression of eating the forbidden fruit was committed by persons who were already wicked.

Adam disobeying God, could not obey himself. [He knew] the misery of being unable to live as he wished.

AUGUSTINE

Abstinence from the fruit of one tree was a kind of first lesson in obedience that man might know he had a Director and Lord of his life.

Adam was constituted a public person . . . a compound of the whole world.

Unbelief was the root defection. Hence flowed ambition and pride . . . also monstrous ingratitude.

JOHN CALVIN

The sin of Adam consisted in this — that he who was naturally every way under the law, and subject to it, would be every way above the law, and no way obliged by it.

A universal rectitude of nature, consisting in light, power, and order, in his understanding, mind and affections, was the principal part of this image of God wherein man was created.

JOHN OWEN

Our father Adam left his whole family with a conscience full of guilt, and a heart full of unsatisfied desires.

THOMAS BOSTON

ADOPTION

Adoption [is] a change of family, a new relationship toward God.

ANON.

He [Jesus] was born the only Son of God, and was unwilling to remain alone.

AUGUSTINE

That we are accounted [God's] children is owing only to the gift of adoption by which He admits us into an union with Him.

God's adoption extends beyond death.

Let us forget all that we have in ourselves, and let us begin with the adoption of God.

JOHN CALVIN

ADOPTION
(CONTINUED)

We are not heirs by nature, but by adoption because it pleased God to take us for His children . . . Are we heirs? Then are we saved.

God can well enough skill [is well able] to discern the mark of His Son . . . We bear the blood of our Lord Jesus Christ for our badge.

The title of 'Son' belongs to Him alone by right, but is placed upon us through grace because God has chosen to adopt us for the sake of His Son.

His adopting of us is to the end that our lives should be blessed and happy, and that after He has preserved us in this world, the inheritance of the heavenly kingdom should be bestowed upon us . . . The true happiness of men is to have the favour and love of God.

An unfeigned love of God's law is an undoubted evidence of adoption since this love is the work of the Holy Spirit.

When we are about assurance of salvation, then we must call to mind the free adoption alone, which is joined with the expiation and forgiveness of sins.

When it pleases Him to imprint the certainty of his promises in our hearts by his Holy Spirit; then is it a special adoption.

God's will is that we should resemble Him, because He has adopted us for His children.

JOHN CALVIN

By regeneration we are made members of God's kingdom (*John* 3:35); by adoption members of His family (*Gal.* 4:5,6).

JOHN MURRAY

AMBITION – FALSE

Men seek nothing so much as to make themselves seem something.

Teachers . . . have no plague more to be dreaded than ambition.

Greed and ambition . . . the two sources from which stems the corruption of the whole ministry.

Ambition, the foolish wish to be exalted above other men, is the deadliest plague that a person entrusted with the responsibility to teach others could ever have.

JOHN CALVIN

AMBITION – TRUE

I have hitherto lived to little purpose, more like a clod than a servant of God; now let me burn out for God.

HENRY MARTYN, on arriving in India, 1805

Give me the love that leads the
way,
The faith that nothing can dismay,
The hope no disappointments tire,
The passion that will burn like
fire.
Let me not sink to be a clod.
Make me Thy fuel, Flame of God!

AMY WILSON CARMICHAEL

I think if I have any ambition, it
is just this – to have honourable
mention in anyone's personal relationship with our Lord Jesus Christ.

OSWALD CHAMBERS

Do not desire to be strong, powerful, honoured and respected; but
let God alone be your strength,
your fame, your honour.

DIETRICH BONHOEFFER

My ambition now is very feeble,
compared with former days; to
win souls and to know God more,
and then to be in the kingdom, is
all my desire.

ANDREW BONAR

When a man says, 'You can't', it
always make me want to prove I
can.

D. L. MOODY

Brethren, be filled with great
ambition; not for yourselves but for
your Lord. Elevate your ideal!
Believe for great things of a great
God.

CHARLES H. SPURGEON

ANGER

There is a great difference between
the anger that proceeds from godly
zeal, and the anger that any of us is
moved by, either for his own goods,
or for his honour, or for any respect
of his own.

Let us learn to use our anger when
we see God's honour wounded,
and when men go about to darken
or deface His truth; let us be
moved and inflamed at it that we
may show ourselves the children of
God. For we can give no better
proof of it.

Intemperate anger deprives men of
their senses . . . Hatred is nothing
more than inveterate anger.

Anger is always our near neighbour.

JOHN CALVIN

One man may be a lamb in private
wrongs, but in hearing general
affronts to goodness, they are asses
which are not lions.

Anger is one of the sinews of the
soul . . . This anger is either heavenly, or hellish, or earthly.

THOMAS FULLER

The emotions of indignation and
anger belong to the very self-
expression of a moral being as such
and cannot be lacking in him in the
presence of wrong.

B. B. WARFIELD

ANTICHRIST

The name antichrist does not designate a single individual, but a single kingdom which extends throughout many generations.

Eusebius cites Jude, c.200 AD, who believed the much talked-of appearance of antichrist would take place at any moment, so completely had the persecutions (under Severus) thrown many off their balance.

Roman antichrist invites us to himself, under the pretence of unity, and pronounces all to be schismatics who do not spontaneously submit to the yoke of his tyranny.

All the marks by which the Spirit of God has pointed out antichrist, clearly appear in the Pope.

JOHN CALVIN

The chief thing I am condemned for as an heretic is because I deny transubstantiation, which is the darling of the devil and daughter and heir to antichrist's religion.

JOHN BRADFORD

Antichrist's bishops preach not but as the disguised bishops mumble, so are their pretentious sacraments dumb.

WILLIAM TYNDALE

ASSURANCE

If because we have the 'first instalment' we cry 'Abba, Father', what will happen when on rising, we see Him face to face?

IRENAEUS

To believers a persuasion of God's fatherly love is more delightful than all earthly enjoyment.

When God shines into us by His Spirit, He at the same time causes the sacred truth which endures forever to shine forth in the mirror of His Word.

The certainty which rests on God's Word exceeds all knowledge.

Would we be assured of our salvation? We must resort not only to God's grace but also chiefly to the promises whereby He utters His love towards us.

If there be no certainty in our religion we will make cold work of it.

The change which we perceive in ourselves now is an infallible witness of the heavenly glory which we see not yet . . . But God gives us a good earnest penny of it . . . the Holy Ghost . . . He is not idle in us but shows openly that He dwells in us.

There is only one way to have assurance of salvation: that is, to realize we are condemned, and to

---

be satisfied that the blood of the Lord Jesus Christ alone can wash and cleanse us . . . It is almost as if the Word of God must be written in red letters in the blood of our Lord Jesus Christ.

JOHN CALVIN

The devil goes about nothing so much as to bring you in doubt, whether you be God's child or no.

JOHN BRADFORD

The waters between here and heaven may all be ridden if we be well horsed; I mean, if we be in Christ.

Believe under a cloud, and wait for Him when there is no moonlight or starlight.

Many have pardon with God who have not peace with themselves.

I am put often to ask if Christ and I did ever shake hands together in earnest.

SAMUEL RUTHERFORD

'Thy sins are forgiven thee', is the only music to the distressed conscience.

ROBERT LEIGHTON

It is in the view of the glory of Christ that we are made partakers of evangelical peace, consolation, joy and assurance.

Without the diligent exercise of the grace of obedience we shall never enjoy the grace of consolation.

JOHN OWEN

On the day before receiving sentence, I met with a great measure and a full gale of the Spirit, wherein my heart was both melted and enlarged, getting near to Him.

JAMES ROBERTSON,
Covenanter; hanged, Edinburgh,
15 December 1682

Assurance is very necessary to enable us for the practice of holiness.

Assurance is more rarely professed by Christians in these times than formerly . . . [this experience] was one of the chief engines whereby the Reformers prevailed to overthrow the Popish superstition.

WALTER MARSHALL

'My brother, have you the witness within yourself? Does the Spirit of God witness with your spirit that you are a child of God?' I was surprised and knew not what to answer. He observed it and asked, 'Do you know Jesus Christ?' I paused and said, 'I know he is the Saviour of the world.' 'True,' he replied, but do you know he has saved you?' I answered, I hope he has died to save me.' He only added, 'Do you know yourself?' I said, 'I do.' But I fear they were vain words.

JOHN WESLEY, on his conversation
with Spangenberg, the Moravian,
7 February 1736.

ASSURANCE

(Continued)

Assurance is not to be obtained so much by self-examination as by action.

Jonathan Edwards

Let us seek to have well-grounded marks of saintship. But when the push comes nothing but imputed righteousness will stand the day.

John Duncan

So long as we ourselves have not entered the New Jerusalem, our comfort should never be founded upon our sanctification, but exclusively upon our justification.

Abraham Kuyper

The simplest believer will always be more sure about divine realities than a doctor of theology deprived – alas, from birth – of that optical organ which is faith.

Auguste Lecerf

I possess assurance only so long as I see these two things simultaneously: all of my sinfulness, and all of God's grace.

Ole Hallesby

Every brand of theology that is not grounded in the particularism which is exemplified in sovereign election and effective redemption is not hospitable to this doctrine of the assurance of faith.

John Murray

ATONEMENT[1]

No type of Christ is more precious, more exact, or more evident than that of the Paschal Lamb.

Zwingli

It is our wisdom to have a clear understanding how much our salvation cost the Son of God.

God at no time received men to mercy without sacrifices.

True it is that the effect of His death comes not to the whole world. Nevertheless . . . it behoves us to labour to bring every man to salvation, that the grace of our Lord Jesus Christ may be available to them.

The whole accomplishment of our salvation and all the parts of it, are contained in His death.

By Christ's obedience He has wiped off our transgressions; by His sacrifice appeased the divine anger; by His blood washed away our stains; by His cross borne our curse; and by His death made satisfaction for us.

John Calvin

Mighty was the malady that needed such a medicine.

John Bradford

[1] See also Jesus Christ – Obedience and Death

The Atonement of Jesus Christ [is] . . . the most honourable treasure of the church, the seed of a blessed immortality and the darling jewel of our religion.

The design of Christ, when He takes believers into union with Himself, is to purge and cleanse them absolutely and perfectly.

The blood-shedding of Jesus Christ accomplished (1) Reconciliation (2) Justification (3) Sanctification (4) Adoption (5) Immortality or eternal redemption.

JOHN OWEN

I have had a desperate dislike of that doctrine; yet now I cannot help feeling that it lies at the foundation of all rightful, solid relief from that dreadful thing, SIN.

JOHN DUNCAN

The doctrine of the atonement . . . the central truth of Christianity and the great theme of Scripture.

The righteousness of God in Romans is a descriptive name for the atonement.

Apart from the atonement, preaching would have no foundation . . . no message to proclaim.

The right to send the Spirit into the hearts of fallen men was acquired by atonement.

The influence of the atonement in procuring the gift of the Holy Spirit . . . There is a special connection between His atoning work and the gift of the Holy Ghost – such a link, in fact, as is established between merit and reward.

There is no motive to a holy life so powerful and efficacious as that which is drawn from the propitiatory work of Christ.

The fall and the atonement constitute the two facts or pivots of human history.

The atonement . . . the grand distinctive peculiarity of the Christian religion.

GEORGE SMEATON

Sinless sin-bearing . . . the descriptive formula for the atonement.

ADOLPH SAPHIR

He is made all our sin as truly as He has none of His own; we are made all His righteousness, as truly as we have none of ours. It is we, wholly and completely, that are His sin; He, wholly and completely, who is our righteousness.

Pardon cannot be understood unless we distinguish the guilt and demerit of sin from its dominion and defilement . . . It is only by pardon that guilt can be cancelled; not by repentance, or even by regeneration.

HUGH MARTIN

ATONEMENT

(CONTINUED)

What you are going to be will make no atonement for what you have been.

CHARLES H. SPURGEON

Aversion to the Atonement is the fruit of pride, self-righteousness and unbelief, which deify man, deny the need of expiation and defy judgment.

The substitution of Christ is described in the Bible, not as a literary illustration, but as a holy reality.

OLE HALLESBY

In the economy of salvation only God's Son had blood to shed and life to lay down in death.

It is by virtue of what Christ has done that the action of both the Father and the Spirit take effect . . . The bearing of Jesus' death and resurrection upon sanctification has not been sufficiently appreciated.

The vicarious sin-bearing of Jesus is that which brought the reconciliation into being.

JOHN MURRAY

The cheapening of Christianity [is] due to the virtual disappearance of the doctrine of the atonement.

In Gethsemane Christ drank the 'cup of the LORD's fury' (*Isa.* 51:22),

and so experienced the sum-total of sin's outrage against the holiness of God.

R.V.G. TASKER

ATONEMENT AND THE HOLY SPIRIT

The right to send the Spirit into the hearts of fallen men was acquired by atonement . . . the Holy Spirit was never spoken of as sent while the old economy stood.

The Holy Spirit was for a time shut up and limited to Christ's own Person. But when the atonement was consummated, the life principle of his own Person was also to be that of His kingdom.

Much loose thinking and unsound doctrine are always associated when the Spirit's work within is made to eclipse or overshadow the Redeemer's finished work without.

GEORGE SMEATON

The great result of [Christ's] atoning death was the power of bestowing the Spirit on others, a blessing so momentous that it may be described as that in which all other blessings are included.

JOHN CALVIN

AUTHORITARIANISM

You [Erasmus] make us defer uncritically to human authority. Where does God's written Word tell us to do that?

MARTIN LUTHER

All the authority that is possessed by pastors is subject to the Word of God.

Whatever authority and dignity is attributed by the Holy Spirit in the Scripture to the priests and prophets under the law, or to the apostles and their successors, it is all given, not in a strict sense to the persons themselves, but to the ministry over which they were appointed, or to speak more correctly, to the Word, the ministration of which was committed to them.

JOHN CALVIN

BACKSLIDING

We must not think it strange if, of a great number of them who were called to the Gospel, there be a very few who continue and stand fast in it . . . It has been so in all times.

You shall see a great number who become cold when God has once given them goods.

Every straw is enough to stay us in this world, and in the meantime we have no mind of the heavenly life.

The more a man shall lift up himself, the further he shall go from God.

The more anyone excels in grace, the more ought he to be afraid of falling.

Slothfulness gradually prevails over the faithful unless it be corrected.

It is requisite that God should put His hand under us, or else our falls would be deadly.

JOHN CALVIN

There is as much need to watch over grace as to watch over sin.

SAMUEL RUTHERFORD

A temporary faith can never save a man, but, on the contrary, it injures him; for it causes his soul to fester.

ABRAHAM KUYPER

There is no more certain forerunner of spiritual shipwreck than the neglect of the written Word.

J. ELDER CUMMING

This loss of spiritual appetite is an evidence of the decay of all other graces.

The work of recovering backsliders from under their spiritual decays, is an act of sovereign grace, wrought in us by virtue of divine promises.

JOHN OWEN

Many came amongst them for a while, who in time of temptation fell away. The displeasure of a tutor . . . the changing of a gown to a higher degree; above all, a thirst for the praise of men, caused numbers shamefully to look back.

GEORGE WHITEFIELD,
on the Holy Club at Oxford.

BAPTISM

[*Baptism in the church at the time of Augustine*] The candidate stood in the baptistry, facing the west, and stretched forth his hands and renounced Satan, as if he were present.

AUGUSTINE

In baptism we have God's own covenant ingraven as it were in our bodies.

The offspring of believers are born holy because their children, while yet in the womb are included in the covenant of eternal life . . . Nor are they admitted into the Church by baptism on any other ground than that they belonged to the body of Christ before they were born.

JOHN CALVIN

The covenant sign [baptism] belongs to the family rather than the individual.

G. W. BROMILEY

BEAUTY

Elegance of form was the occasion of great calamity to holy Joseph . . . Satan is accustomed to turn the gifts of God into snares whereby to catch souls.

JOHN CALVIN

It is a terrible problem – a beautiful face with no true moral beauty below.

FORBES ROBINSON

Aesthetic religion is the offspring of sentiment divorced from law; and that is an illegal divorce.

JOHN DUNCAN

During the history of civilization the sense of beauty, like moral sense, grows, reaches its optimum, declines and disappears.

ALEXIS CARRELL

The gratification of the sense of beauty has never been an influential motive in the activities of Calvinism, because of the conviction that if the thrill caused by human art creations is mistaken for the presence of God, religious and moral degradation follow.

EVANGELICAL QUARTERLY, 1932.

THE BIBLE [1]

The more carnal and worldly a man is the more he has to bring up against the Word of God.

MARTIN LUTHER

When we have departed from the Word of God, though we may suppose that we are firmly established; still ruin is at hand, for our salvation is bound up with the Word of God.

Nothing is more abominable in the sight of God than the contempt of divine truth; for His majesty which shines forth in His Word, is thereby trampled under foot.

[1] See also HOLY SCRIPTURE

[*On Acts 18:6*] God is sorer displeased with contempt of His Word than with any wickedness.

It is the native property of the divine Word never to make its appearance without disturbing Satan, and rousing his opposition.

JOHN CALVIN

Whatever contradicts the Word of God should be instantly resisted as diabolical.

JOHN BUNYAN

The plenary inspiration of the Scriptures may be called a question of existence for the Protestant Church.

GEORGE SMEATON

We receive the Bible because of Christ, and we receive Christ through the Bible.

The same Spirit convinces us of the supremacy of Christ and of the supremacy of Scripture.

ADOLPH SAPHIR

Do not try to make the Bible relevant. Its relevance is axiomatic . . . Do not defend God's Word, but testify to it . . . Trust to the Word.

DIETRICH BONHOEFFER, to his students, early in World War II

BIBLE STUDY [1]

Scripture is not in our power, nor in the ability of our mind. There-

[1] See also MEMORIZING SCRIPTURE

fore, in its study we must in no way rely on our own understanding, but we must become humble, and pray that He may bring that understanding to us.

MARTIN LUTHER

God's Word has the nature and property so to strengthen us as we shall no more be feeble.

The Holy Spirit so adheres to His own truth that He only displays and exerts His power where the Word is received with due reverence and honour.

All who desire to be instructed in the Word of God shall know His will by the same, neither will He suffer them to err, or to be deceived.

One rule of modesty and sobriety [is] not to speak or think, or even desire to know concerning obscure subjects, anything beyond the information given us in the Divine Word.

JOHN CALVIN

Apply thyself wholly to the text. Apply the subject wholly to thyself.

J. A. BENGEL

Let everyone that desires to be not merely a so-called theologian or divine, but taught of God — a true disciple and lover of God — resolve within himself above all things to make this sacred volume

BIBLE STUDY

(CONTINUED)

his constant study, intermingling his reading with frequent and fervent prayer; for if this be omitted, his labour will be altogether in vain, supposing him to be ever so well versed in these books and to have besides all the advantages that can be had from the knowledge of languages and the assistance of commentators.

ROBERT LEIGHTON

Which is the best commentary on the Bible? The Bible itself.

SAMUEL WESLEY

Reverential reading includes attention, exertion of mind, and earnestness. Not memory but conscience; not intellect but the heart . . . can enable us to use Scripture aright.

ADOLPH SAPHIR

I have always thought that some knowledge of the Bible is necessary to an understanding of English history. Certainly the intensive private study of that book by many hundreds of thousands of persons otherwise unlearned, had more to do with the character, the mind and the imaginative power of our ancestors than we moderns can always understand.

G. M. TREVELYAN

The principle that everyone must learn to read in order to understand the Bible for himself is the most important contribution of the Reformation to education.

M. C. V. JEFFREYS

I have sometimes seen more in a line of Scripture than I could well tell how to stand under, and yet at another time the whole Bible has been to me as a dry stick.

JOHN BUNYAN

Thereby [that is, through Bible reading] did the knowledge of God wondrously increase, and God gave His Holy Spirit to simple men in great abundance.

JOHN KNOX

I am particularly convinced of my sin of superficial reading of the Scripture, not subjecting my soul, in reading, unto it, as the divine Word; whereby it has come to pass I have not had the feeling of the power of it.

THOMAS BOSTON

My mind being now more open . . . I began to read the Holy Scriptures upon my knees, laying aside all other books, and praying over, if possible every line and word.

I get more true knowledge by reading the Book of God in one month than I could ever have acquired from all the writings of men.

GEORGE WHITEFIELD

For many, many years I have never read my Bible without having a

A – Z OF CHRISTIAN TRUTH AND EXPERIENCE

scribbling pad either on my table or in my pocket.

D. MARTYN LLOYD-JONES

Any study of God's Word which is merely intellectual uniformly endangers the Word's vital power and continual handling of it thus becomes, very often, fatal to the individual.

S. R. McPHAIL

BURIAL

Burial was brought in by God; it is no invention of man. It is God's ordinance, a witness to us of the resurrection and eternal life. Immoderate funeral expenses quench the sweet savour of Christ's resurrection.

JOHN CALVIN

It was the universal custom of the Jews to bury their dead . . . After a few Roman Emperors had received baptism there was not a body burnt in all the Roman Empire.

The decent custom of the primitive Christians [that is, burial of the dead] was so acceptable to God that by His providence it proved most effectual in the conversion of the heathen and the propagation of the Gospel.

Julian the Apostate [331–63], no friend of Christianity, reckoned three influences by which Christianity gained upon the pagan world:

1. The gravity of their behaviour;
2. their kindness to strangers;
3. their care for the burial of the dead.

JOHN PEARSON

Jesus has left the tomb nothing but his winding sheet.

HENRY LIDDON

CHASTISEMENT

God grants this privilege to His elect – that He chastises them paternally as His children, while He deals with the reprobate as a severe judge, so that all the punishments which they endure are fatal . . . God acts as a Father towards His elect, and as a judge towards the reprobate.

JOHN CALVIN

CHARISMATIC GIFTS
SEE GIFTS

CHRISTIANS

A Christian man is a spiritual thing, and has God's Word in his heart, and God's Spirit to certify him of all things.

WILLIAM TYNDALE

The nature of Christianity [is] conformity with Christ and . . . disconformity with the world.

ROBERT LEIGHTON

Christians are Christlike; none deserves the name of Christian who is not so in his prevailing character.

JONATHAN EDWARDS

CHRISTIAN MINISTRY

Let him who wants to counsel others faithfully, first have some experience himself, first carry the cross himself, and lead the way by his example.

MARTIN LUTHER

Either teach not, or teach by living.

GREGORY NAZIANZEN

Although all of us, from the most to the least, be priests, yet . . . it is the duty of the ministers of the Word to teach and to show men the way to God.

This secret call . . . is the honest testimony of our heart, that we accept the office offered to us, not from ambition or avarice, or any other unlawful motive but from a sincere fear of God and an ardent zeal for the edification of the church.

The ministry of men, which God employs in His government of the church, is the principal bond which holds believers together in one body.

Let the minister attempt nothing trusting in his own wit and industry, but let him commit his labour to the Lord, upon whose grace the whole success depends.

When ministers are lowered, contempt of the Word arises.

The government of the church by the preaching of the Word is declared to be no human contrivance, but a most sacred ordinance of Christ . . . They who despise or reject this ministry offer insult and rebellion to Christ the Author.

There are no regular teachers but those on whom God has conferred this office.

We ought to make so great account of the calling of God, that no unthankfulness of men may be able to hinder us.

[*On 1 Timothy 3:6*] They which are to govern His church must not be younglings . . . A man must be well fashioned and have run a good race a long while. Not only is strength and vigour of body requisite for spiritual warfare, but seriousness and gravity also. If they had been admitted in their youth their levity might have detracted from the reverence due to sacred things.

A shepherd must settle in a certain place and he must tarry there as if he were fast bound.

Let not men cease to have preachers of God's Word and ministers of His sacraments still: for otherwise it were the next way to cut the church's throat, and to bring all to utter desolation.

If there be a man chosen to preach God's Word, and God be minded to show favour to His Church, He will endue that man with His Spirit, He will give him understanding of His Word, and He will grant him cunning and skill to apply it to the use of the people and to gather good doctrine of it, and He will give him jealousness and all other things that are requisite.

A man shall never be meet to be a teacher, unless he has put on a fatherly affection.

No man shall ever be a good minister of God's Word unless he be a scholar first.

He is no more his own man, nor at his own choice . . . He must dedicate himself wholly to God.

There are very few of those who bear the title of ministers in the present day, who have the mark of sincerity impressed on them . . . The consequence is that no majesty of God is seen in their ministry.

Private men indeed sin; but in pastors there is the blame of negligence and still more, when they deviate even the least from the right way, a greater offence is given.

JOHN CALVIN

All churches rise or fall as the ministry doth rise or fall.

A man must love God above all before he can heartily serve God before all.

When the people see that you unfeignedly love them, they will hear anything, and bear anything, and follow you the more easily.

RICHARD BAXTER

Untender, unskilful and unfaithful men may creep in and be admitted to the ministry . . . No man wounds the Church more . . . than a gifted untender minister may do.

JAMES DURHAM

The first and most urgent cry of the people when light began to dawn upon them was for preachers.

WILLIAM CUNNINGHAM

God save us from the men of willow and gutta–percha and plaster of paris . . . Take them away, O Father Time, and give us back men of granite, men of backbone, say rather, men of God!

CHARLES H. SPURGEON

Without believing in and knowing something of the power of the Spirit [the ministry] is a heartbreaking task.

D. MARTYN LLOYD-JONES

THE CHURCH

According then to this divine foreknowledge and predestination, how many sheep are outside, and how many wolves within! And how many sheep are inside, how many wolves without!

AUGUSTINE

THE CHURCH

(CONTINUED)

What is the church? The body and society of believers whom God hath predestined to eternal life.

Churches easily decay . . . unless they be looked to continually.

If at this day we perceive the church to decrease, yea, even so far as it may seem to be nothing, let us understand that God will multiply it, seeing he has made that promise.

When there are great troubles and confusions in his church, let us remember that our Lord Jesus Christ reigns.

The life of the church is not without a resurrection, nay, it is not without many resurrections.

He will guide his church. But this is not to say that he will guard it in the way we might imagine. It is often necessary that he raise the dead; it is necessary that he create a new people (*Psa*.102:18).

We shall often see that the kingdom of our Lord Jesus Christ shall seem to be abolished out of the world.

JOHN CALVIN

I am sorry for our desolate kirk; yet I dare not but trust, so long as there be any of God's lost money here, He shall not blow out the candle.

SAMUEL RUTHERFORD

The exercise of discipline in the church is 'an evidence and pledge of the future judgment'.

JOHN OWEN

The church has three kinds of enemies: the Jews who have never been of her body; the heretics who have withdrawn from it; and bad Christians who rend her from within.

BLAISE PASCAL

In the Apostles Creed the church is 'the communion of saints' . . . The church is not essentially a visible society. The unity of the church is threefold: (1) spiritual (2) comprehensive, embracing all the people of God (3) historical, the same in all ages.

CHARLES HODGE

CHURCH HISTORY

[Certain of] those whom we call 'the Early Church Fathers' . . . distorted the plain meaning of Holy Scripture. They were bewitched by Satan himself.

The perpetuity of the life of the Risen Jesus is the guarantee of the perpetuity of the Christian church . . . Christ's superiority to the assaults of death is the secret of His church's immortality.

JOHN CALVIN

The history of the church is nothing less than the history of the Risen

Christ conquering the world through the body in which he lives.

BROOKE FOSS WESCOTT

I know of nothing which is a greater tonic to me in my Christian life than to read the lives of the saints. You can never read too much of such literature. Read about such men as David Brainerd, Jonathan Edwards, Robert Murray M'Cheyne. Go after them, my friends, spare no effort to acquire them.

D. MARTYN LLOYD-JONES

COMMUNION OF SAINTS

The saints of God living in the church of Christ are in communion with all the saints departed out of this life and admitted to the presence of God. The mystical union between Christ and his church is the true foundation of that communion which one member has with another. They fellowship with all the saints who from the death of Abel have departed in the true faith and fear of God and now enjoy the presence of the Father, and follow the Lamb whithersoever he goeth.

JOHN PEARSON

All the saints of paradise acknowledge us as their brethren, and embrace us for our Lord Jesus Christ's sake.

If another man have more gracious gifts than I, I am rich in his person,

for when we confess the communion of saints it is to show that whatsoever God gives to one man, or to another, redounds to the benefit of all.

JOHN CALVIN

Christianity has created a vast brotherhood, and the fellowship which this brotherhood inspires is the true communion of saints.

HENRY SWETE

CONSCIENCE

There is a tribunal erected in every man, where conscience is accuser, witness and judge.

THOMAS BOSTON

A sensitive conscience is a precious defence for the believer.

OLE HALLESBY

The idea of conscience was unknown to heathenism.

ALFRED EDERSHEIM

God has taken the conscience of the godly under the government of his Word, and claims this as his right.

It is a pernicious evil to exercise an arbitrary control over the conscience.

What is the chief welfare of man? To be sure that his conscience is quiet and at rest, so as he may go on in true constancy, through life, and through death, yes, and even be merry.

JOHN CALVIN

CONSCIENCE
(Continued)

Those build for hell who build against their conscience.

When we do not know whether God has permitted a thing, we dare not budge a finger lest our conscience become seared as with a hot iron.

There is not a worse thing than to have our consciences asleep.

All are rendered inexcusable, as they carry in their hearts a law which is sufficient to make them a thousand times guilty.

Our consciences will never enjoy peace till they rest on the propitiation for sins.

JOHN CALVIN

Conscience is pacified by nothing which does not pacify the justice of God.

GEORGE SMEATON

CONSECRATION

By the example of Abraham, entire self-renunciation is enjoined, that we may live and die to God alone.

We are linked to our Lord Jesus Christ that he might dedicate us to the Father.

JOHN CALVIN

[The Christian] renews this gift of himself every day to God, and receiving it every day, bettered again, still he has the more delight in giving it, as being fitter for God.

ROBERT LEIGHTON

New washing, renewed application of purchased redemption, by that sacred blood which sealeth the free covenant, is a thing of daily and hourly use to a poor sinner.

SAMUEL RUTHERFORD

All I am and have, both in principle and practice, is to be summed up in the one expression, the Lord's property'.

J. A. BENGEL

It is the presentation or giving away of all we have to God and our taking simply the place of servants, to receive back again just what he chooses. This, it will be perceived, if a reality, is no easy task and can only be done in the might of the Holy Ghost; but, when it is done, when all is laid on the altar — body, soul, spirit, goods, reputation, all, all, all — then the fire of heaven descends and burns up all the dross and defilement, and fills the souls with burning love and zeal and power.

WILLIAM BOOTH

CONTROVERSY

Satan knows that nothing is more fit to lay waste to the kingdom of

Christ than discord and disagreement among the faithful.

If the devil go about to kindle strife and debate in all places, out of doubt he will begin with the ministers of the Word.

JOHN CALVIN

A man, though he err, if he do it calmly and meekly, may be a better man than he who is stormily and furiously orthodox . . . I would sound a retreat from our unnatural contentions and irreligious strivings for religion. Oh! what are the things we fight for, compared with the great things of God? God forbid any should think that except all be according to our mind, we must break the bond of peace.

ROBERT LEIGHTON

A dead calm is our enemy, a storm may prove our helper. Controversy may arouse thought, and through thought may come the Divine change.

CHARLES H. SPURGEON

When a great and true revival comes in the church, the present miserable, feeble talk about avoidance of controversy on the part of the servants of Jesus Christ will all be swept away as with a mighty flood. A man who is really on fire with his message never talks in that feeble and compromising way.

J. GRESHAM MACHEN

CONVERSION

A resurrection before a resurrection.

When we turn to God He helps us; when we turn away from Him He forsakes us.

To pass from death to life is to pass from unbelief to faith, from injustice to justice, from pride to humility, from hatred to charity.

To heal our souls God uses all kinds of means.

AUGUSTINE

The word conversion, or turning, imports that whereas man has turned his back on God, he must turn again toward him with his face.

[On the dying thief] Drawn from hell to heaven . . . he adores Christ as king while on the gallows, and declared Him, when dying, to be the author of life . . . He beheld life in death, exaltation in ruin, glory in shame, victory in destruction, a kingdom in bondage.

He begins at love, to the intent to draw us unto Him after a loving manner, and not by force.

To win God's favour . . . all that is needed is simple confession of our sins and faith.

JOHN CALVIN

CONVERSION

Until God has tamed us, we are both deaf and blind, yes, and in a manner lunatic.

[*On Zacchaeus*] Before revealing Himself to men, the Lord frequently communicates to them a secret desire, by which they are led to Him, while He is still concealed and unknown . . . drawn to Him by a secret movement of the Spirit . . . He is never sought in vain by those who sincerely desire to know Him . . . This must be regarded as the beginning of faith.

The conversion of men comes not from themselves, nor of their own strength nor of their own moving; it is God who reforms them, who makes them new creatures; God reserves the conversion of sinners to Himself.

Conversion cannot be separated from prayer.

Our Lord so works in his elect that, after he has humbled them, they suffer themselves to be led without any more resistance, insomuch that their whole pleasure and joy is to be subject to God.

It belongs only to God to alter men's hearts.

God does not wait for us to come to him, but he takes the pains of coming to seek us.

No mortal ever approaches God without being divinely drawn.

JOHN CALVIN

Christ beginneth young with many, and stealeth into their heart ere they wit of themselves, and becometh homely with them, with little din or noise.

SAMUEL RUTHERFORD

Most persons are effectually converted to God, and have saving faith, whereby they believe the Scripture, and virtually all that is contained in it, before they have ever once considered them.

JOHN OWEN

As from every point of the circumference of a circle we may imagine straight lines converging to the centre, not one of which is exactly coincident with another, so is each individual drawn towards God by a way more or less peculiar to that individual.

J. A. BENGEL

Probably no two persons in believing have precisely the same truths, in all their relations, presented to them.

ARCHIBALD ALEXANDER

To be converted is to transfer our life's centre of gravity from ourselves to God, to free ourselves from ourselves, to break with our self-sufficient and selfish nature, and to seek our supreme satisfaction not in ourselves but in him.

CHRISTOPH LUTHARDT

The work of conversion consists to two parts: (1) the well-informing of the judgment of the necessary points; (2) the change of the will, by the efficacy of the truth.

RICHARD BAXTER

The Holy Spirit works on the *world* for conviction (*John* 16:8), on the *elect* for conversion.

JOHN OWEN

It is profitable for Christians to be often calling to mind the very beginnings of grace with their souls.

JOHN BUNYAN

True conversion most frequently consists of four stages: first the head, secondly the heart, thirdly the mouth and fourth the pocket.

ANON.

A sinner does not 'decide' for Christ; the sinner 'flies' to Christ in utter helplessness and despair.

D. MARTYN LLOYD-JONES

CONVICTIONS

He stands like a rock because he has first taken care to stand on a rock.

W. M. TAYLOR

The cult of an open mind is a way of camouflaging the poverty of an education which has no view of life to communicate.

M. C. V. JEFFREYS

There will be no persuasiveness of speech that can turn aside the minds of those that have devoted their understanding to Christ.

We must be absolutely determined to suffer for the doctrines we preach.

If we have not this godly zeal towards God's truth we show ourselves to be none of his children.

JOHN CALVIN

COURAGE

I desire not to go on the lee-side or sunny side of religion, or to put truth betwixt me and the storm. My Saviour, in his suffering, took the windy side of the hill.

SAMUEL RUTHERFORD

THE COVENANT

The covenant imports that first and foremost God receives us to mercy, even without finding anything but utter cursedness in us. And secondly, that He continues His favour towards us for love of His only Son. And thirdly, that He accepts our works and takes them for good . . . and all by virtue of the said covenant.

This word is limited to those 'contracts' by which the Lord, who adopted His people, promised that He would be their God . . . The

THE COVENANT
(Continued)

chief part of the word consists of promises by which He adopts and receives us as His own.

The covenant was founded on Christ alone.

Whenever the word 'covenant' appears in Scripture we ought to recall to remembrance the word 'grace'.

He our God, we His inheritance; He our King, we His people; we His children, He our Father.

JOHN CALVIN

As Satan labours to loosen our faith, so must we labour to fasten it, by thinking on the promises and covenant of God in Christ's blood.

JOHN BRADFORD

Stand upon the advance ground of the promises and the covenant of grace.

ROBERT LEIGHTON

The main theme of the Bible is the covenant-relationship between God and man.

R. V. G. TASKER

It is the promise of unreserved fidelity, of whole-souled commitment that appears to constitute the essence of the covenant . . . It is not compact or contract which provides the constitutive or governing idea but that of dispensation in the sense of disposition . . . When we remember that covenant is not only bestowment of grace, not only oath-bound promise, but also relationship to God in that which is the crown and goal of the whole process of religion, namely, union and communion with God, we discover again that the new covenant brings this relationship also to the highest level of achievement. At the centre of covenant revelation as its constant refrain is the assurance, 'I will be your God, and ye shall be my people.'

JOHN MURRAY

CREEDS

It is a deeply significant historical fact that the two great creed-producing eras of the church, the era of the Fathers and the era of the Reformation, were times when the Scriptures, through fresh study and earnest investigation, literally had free course.

W. A. CURTIS

No rational being can be creedless.

ROBERT FLINT

CRITICISM

Do not be fond of criticizing others, and do not resent their criticism of you.

EPICTETUS

We are so fascinated with the malignant pleasure of examining and detecting the faults of others.

The disease and lust of detraction [whereby]. . . every man who hurts his neighbour violates the fundamental law of human society.

JOHN CALVIN

An overweening esteem that men naturally have of themselves mounts them in the censor's chair.

ROBERT LEIGHTON

Generally speaking, an immunity from criticism is to be secured by inefficiency, feebleness, or disloyalty to principle, on the part of the teacher.

HENRY LIDDON

DANGER

[There is] no greater danger than no danger at all.

MARTIN LUTHER

Very few are strong enough to bear attacks on the gospel.

Shut your eyes against all that will daunt your courage and open your eyes to behold the inestimable power of God.

JOHN CALVIN

DEAD FAITH

Dead faith is a false idea which men entertain about receiving grace although they will not repent.

OLE HALLESBY

DEATH

[*On Hebrews 11:34*] The victory of faith appears more splendid in the contempt of death than if life were extended to the fifth generation. It is more glorious evidence of faith . . . when reproaches, want and extreme troubles are borne with resignation and firmness, than when recovery from sickness is miraculously obtained, or any other benefit from God.

God always ripens His servants before He calls them out of the world, so they are fully satisfied when they come to their graves.

In order that a good conscience may lead us peacefully and quietly to the grave, it is necessary to rely upon the resurrection of Christ, for we then go willingly to God.

JOHN CALVIN

Question: What benefit do believers in Christ receive at death?
Answer: The souls of believers are at their death made perfect in holiness, and do immediately pass into glory; and their bodies, being still united to Christ, do rest in their graves till the resurrection.

WESTMINSTER SHORTER CATECHISM,
Q. AND A. 37

DEPENDENCE ON GOD

When anyone is not exercised with great difficulties in discharging his

DEPENDENCE ON GOD
(Continued)

office of teaching, only a common measure of the Spirit is necessary for the performance of his duties; but when anyone is drawn into arduous and difficult struggles he is at the same time especially strengthened by the Lord.

JOHN CALVIN

THE DEVIL / DEMONS
See Satan

DISUNITY

The impurity and earthiness of men's minds is the great cause of disunion and disaffection among them, and of all their strifes.

ROBERT LEIGHTON

DIVINE MYSTERIES

The mercy by which God freely delivers, and the truth by which He righteously judges, are equally unsearchable.

AUGUSTINE

Whenever we are disturbed at the paucity of believers, let us remember that none, but those to whom it was given, have any apprehension of the mystery of God.

God lisps, as it were, with us, just as nurses are accustomed to speak to infants.

Only fools seek to know the essence of God. The wisdom of the flesh is always exclaiming against the mysteries of God.

In heavenly mysteries the whole power of the human mind is utterly unavailing.

JOHN CALVIN

All false religions pretended always unto things which are mysterious.

JOHN OWEN

My shallow and ebb thoughts are not the compass that my Lord saileth by. I leave His ways to Himself, for they are far, far, above me.

SAMUEL RUTHERFORD

How dark the veil that intercepts
   the blaze
Of heaven's mysterious purposes
   and ways.

WILLIAM COWPER

What he did not understand he refrained from attempting to explain.

DAVID BROWN, on JOHN DUNCAN

Addison and Swift both conjectured, not unwarrantably, in connection with these mysteries (of the Trinity and such like) that new faculties might be given in the life to come to apprehend what is now incomprehensible and unknown.

GEORGE SMEATON

Mystery is the mark which the Infinite Being has placed on his work, and it judges reason. Mystery is the atmosphere necessary to the religious life.

AUGUSTE LECERF

Sin — human sin — is the one great negative mystery of our existence of which we know only one thing, that we are responsible for it, without the possibility of our pushing our responsibility on to anything outside ourselves.

EMIL BRUNNER

DOUBT

Academics doubt everything.

AUGUSTINE

What will he ever learn who is taught to doubt?

MARTIN LUTHER, on ERASMUS

We know our great propensity to doubt.

How shockingly do they insult God, when they doubt his truth! What do you leave to God if you take that from him?

To be submissive is much greater virtue than to be questioning. We are to show Him reverence by closing our mouths and opening our ears to his revelation.

All questions are at an end when we are grounded in the truth of God. For so soon as we shall doubt the Word of God, we cannot choose but be shaken.

JOHN CALVIN

The incredulous are the most credulous.

BLAISE PASCAL

An army of doubters may be the most likely to attack and overcome the town of Mansoul.

Thus they buried in the plains about Mansoul, the Election-Doubters, the Vocation-Doubters, the Grace-Doubters, the Perseverance-Doubters, the Resurrection-Doubters, the Salvation-Doubters and the Glory-Doubters.

JOHN BUNYAN

How difficult is it to get our 'hows' and 'whys' crucified, and to resolve all into, and rest all satisfied in, infinite wisdom tempered with covenant love!

THOMAS BOSTON

Doubts and fears are not marks of God's children. They are remnants of the old nature — specks upon the eye of faith. You should give them no quarter.

If you say it is good to have doubts, you are just saying, ' I will not take all that God offers.' Faith takes a whole Christ for itself: 'My Lord and my God.'

ANDREW BONAR

Some appear to hold that a certain measure of cautious doubt on all subjects is inseparable from true intellectual culture.

HENRY LIDDON

The learned gentlemen are frequently the greatest doubters.

ABRAHAM KUYPER

DOUBT
(CONTINUED)

We reject everything which, when tested by pure reason, appears uncertain. Thus doubt, so far from being the final sin, became the primary virtue.

G. R. CRAGG

EFFECTUAL CALLING

Without His calling we cannot even will.

AUGUSTINE

Men come not to Christ except through the wonderful agency of God . . . The impulse by which God moves the elect to betake themselves to the fold of Christ is supernatural.

God lets His elect ones go for a time, so that they seem to be astray and utterly lost, and yet He brings them home again to His flock when it pleases Him . . . Experience shows that He lets them go astray till the opportune time has come to call them.

The gift of believing is a special gift . . . God effectually calls all whom He has elected so that the sheep of Christ are proved by their faith.

No one will dedicate himself to God until he be drawn by His goodness, and embrace Him with all his heart. He must therefore call us to Him before we call upon Him; we can have no access till He first invite us . . . allured and delighted by the goodness of God.

The blood of Christ is not only the pledge of our salvation, but also the cause of our calling.

JOHN CALVIN

This calling . . . refers to the real bringing of a Christian to Christ, and uniting him with Christ.

ROBERT LEIGHTON

With scarcely an exception, the New Testament means by the words 'call', 'called', 'calling', nothing less than the call which is efficacious unto salvation.

JOHN MURRAY

ELECTION

Election is for the purpose of holiness.

AUGUSTINE

'They shall never perish' (*John* 10:28). This is a remarkable passage by which we are taught that the salvation of all the elect is not less certain than the power of God is invincible . . . In short, our salvation is certain because it is in the hand of God.

Ignorance of this principle evidently detracts from the divine glory, and diminishes real humility . . . they who desire to extinguish this principle pluck up humility by the roots.

The election of God is to give us a sure constancy, to make us merry in the midst of troubles.

Whereupon hangs our salvation? Is it not upon the election and choice that has been from everlasting? God chose us, before we were, and what could we do then?

What is the election of God? It is the fact that before the constitution of the world, He chose us to be His children, in our Lord Jesus Christ.

When we come to election, we see nothing but mercy on every side.

[On Hebrews 2:13] Christ brings none to the Father but those given to Him by the Father; and this donation, we know, depends on eternal election.

It is the election of God alone which makes the difference between some and others.

Let us resort to this election of God as oft soever as we be dismayed by any man's fall.

God's election is one single act; for it is eternal and immutable.

He chooses from among His enemies those whose hearts He bends to the love of Him.

The end of our election is that we may show forth the glory of God in every possible way.

There is not anything which ought to move us more to the serving of God, than to come to the knowledge of our free election.

The paternal favour of God towards the elect is like a fan to excite against them the enmity of the world . . . A blind ferocity impels them to an unintentional resistance against God.

The wickedness of men cannot change the election of God.

How do we know that God has elected us before the creation of the world? By believing in Jesus Christ.

JOHN CALVIN

Why? No man is able to understand, and therefore we should bid our busy brain sit down, and not to covet again to be like God, as Adam did.

JOHN BRADFORD

He that loves may be sure that He was loved first.

ROBERT LEIGHTON

The doctrine of God's eternal election is everywhere in Scripture proposed for the encouragement and consolation of believers, and to further them in their course of obedience and holiness.

JOHN OWEN

ELECTION

(CONTINUED)

Titus was settled in office to bring the elect of God to faith . . . Election is the cause of faith and not faith the cause of election.

STEPHEN CHARNOCK

I admire the doctrine of election . . . It has the natural tendency to rouse the soul out of its carnal security.

I am of the martyr Bradford's mind. Let a man go to the grammar school of faith and repentance, before he goes to the university of election and predestination.

GEORGE WHITEFIELD

There is not a converted and believing man on earth in whose conscience there does not exist, at least the germ, or embryo of a testimony in favour of the substance of the Calvinistic doctrine of election.

WILLIAM CUNNINGHAM

The confession of election and foreordination is essentially the recognition of a grace active long before the hour of conversion.

It has pleased the Lord to lift only a corner of the veil covering this mystery — no more than the Holy Spirit deemed necessary for the support of our faith, for the glory of God and the benefit of others in the hour of their spiritual birth.

ABRAHAM KUYPER

Election is prior to faith, but it is learned by faith.

JOHN MURRAY

END TIMES

As the end of the world approaches errors increase, terrors multiply, iniquity increases: the light . . . charity . . . is very often extinguished, this darkness of enmity between brethren daily increases, and Jesus is not yet come.

AUGUSTINE

ERROR

We must not desire to know more than is contained in his Word. For when men will be wise against God, they become stark mad.

No one can faithfully teach the Church, except he is diligent in banishing errors.

Men are more ready to receive error and vanity than to receive the Word of God.

It is impossible for men to be withdrawn from errors, unless they have God's Word.

No man is qualified to become a teacher of heavenly doctrine unless his feelings respecting it be such that he is distressed and agonized when it is treated with contempt.

JOHN CALVIN

Truth is but one; error is endless and interminable.

ROBERT LEIGHTON

The mischievous notion of the innocence of error . . .

WILLIAM WILBERFORCE

The great source of error in religious matters is that men do not fully and honestly take the Word of God as their rule and standard.

WILLIAM CUNNINGHAM

Sinners purified without penitence, just men sanctified without charity . . . God without power over the will of men, a predestination without mystery, a redemption without certainty . . . Almost everybody has acquired a propensity to believe in falsehoods.

BLAISE PASCAL

By corrupting the true doctrine they are turning meat into poison, life into death, light into darkness.

There was never any poison of false doctrine but it was put into a golden cup.

The omission of fundamental truth is equivalent to the inculcation of deadly error.

They separate God from his Word, the church from faith, and the kingdom of God from the Spirit.

If he who bears the candlestick to light other men reels and stumbles and loses his way, how dreadful that would be.

JOHN CALVIN

Faults in the life breed errors in
    the brain,
And these reciprocally again.
The mind and conduct mutually
    imprint
And stamp their image in each
    other's mint . . .
The pride of lettered ignorance,
    that binds
In chains of error our accomplished
    minds.

WILLIAM COWPER

ETERNITY

'In the morning' (*Psa.*49:14), a beautiful metaphor for the resurrection of the dead –'the morning' which will introduce eternity . . . which points us to a 'day' of extraordinary kind, when God Himself shall rise upon us as the sun, and surprise us with the discovery of His glory.

In this world we taste but the beginning of Christ's kingdom.

We shall never be fit for the service of God if we look not beyond this fleeting life.

JOHN CALVIN

The Rev. Thomas Chalmers, when Church of Scotland minister of Kilmany, Fife, wrote: 'After the satisfactory discharge of his parish duties, a minister may enjoy five days in a week of uninterrupted leisure for the prosecution of any science.'

ETERNITY
(Continued)

Years later, in a debate in the General Assembly he confessed his error in these words: 'I had forgot two magnitudes: I thought not of the littleness of time; I recklessly thought not of the greatness of eternity.'

EVANGELICALISM

That only is true evangelicalism in which sounds clearly the double confession that all the power exerted in saving the soul is from God, and that God in His saving operations acts directly upon the soul.

B. B. WARFIELD

EXAMPLE

This is the artifice of Satan – to seek some misconduct on the part of ministers that may tend to the dishonouring of the gospel.

We see a great number who can talk well enough of the gospel, and yet have nothing but a tongue.

JOHN CALVIN

One proud, surly, lordly word, one needless contention, one covetous action may cut the throat of many a sermon and blast the fruit of all you have been doing.

RICHARD BAXTER

FAITH

Faith is conceived from the Scriptures.
Faith will totter if the authority of Scripture begin to shake.

Faith as well in its beginning as in its completion, is God's gift . . . given to some, while to some it is not given.

The grace of God which both begins a man's faith and which enables it to persevere unto the end, is not given in respect of our merits, but . . . according to His own most sacred and . . . most righteous, wise and beneficial will.

Works proceed from faith, not faith from works.

AUGUSTINE

Faith is a living and unshakeable confidence, a belief in the grace of God, so assured that a man would die a thousand deaths for its sake. This makes us joyful, high-spirited and eager in our relations with God and with all mankind.

MARTIN LUTHER

Faith is a spiritual resurrection of the soul.

It is a signal proof of faith to take light from heaven to guide us to the hope of salvation when we are surrounded in the world with darkness on all sides.

There is no faith without teaching.

Our faith is never perfect; we are partly unbelievers.
Faith is a humble, self-denying grace; it makes the Christian nothing in himself, and all in God.

Faith means such a reformation in ourselves that our life is totally changed.

'To hear' in Scripture, generally means 'to believe'.

A steady and certain knowledge of the divine benevolence towards us, which, being founded on the truth of the gratuitous promise in Christ, is both revealed to our minds and confirmed to our hearts by the Holy Spirit.

Faith . . . the key which opens the gate which leads us to God.

Faith does not proceed from ourselves, but is the fruit of spiritual regeneration.

Faith [is] . . . a lively knowledge, rooted in the heart.

True faith confines its view so entirely to Christ that [it] neither knows, nor desires to know, anything else.

[God] denies [faith] to be the proper effect of human exertion . . . it is a specimen of the Divine power.

Faith has its degrees in beholding Christ.

Faith has its silence to lend an ear to the Word of God.
Our faith increases according to our profiting in the Holy Scriptures.

We must stoop under the Word of God, and faith must be all our understanding.

Faith is the principle of spiritual light and life in us . . . no idle feeling . . . but an energizing principle. No man can obtain faith by his own acuteness, but only by the secret illumination of His Spirit.

There are two things contained in faith: the one is humbleness, the other is glory.

Holiness is the true evidence of our faith.

Faith overrules our affections [feelings].

Faith is not only prompt and ready in obedience, but invigorates and quickens the whole man.

JOHN CALVIN

Faith in Jesus Christ is a saving grace, whereby we receive and rest upon Him alone for salvation as He is offered to us in the gospel.

WESTMINSTER SHORTER CATECHISM,
Answer 86

FAITH

(CONTINUED)

Divine revelation is the proper object of divine faith.

It is in the exercise of faith in Christ that the Holy Spirit puts forth His renewing, transforming power, in and upon our souls.

True faith can no more be without holiness, than true fire without heat.

JOHN OWEN

Faith is a good friend in desertion . . . it speaks good of Christ even behind his back.

JAMES DURHAM

God not only saves upon believing, but gives believing itself.

This solid faith doth empty the believer of himself . . . The native work of faith is to make the soul rest in Christ alone . . . True faith lays the burden of all duties and difficulties upon Him.

BLAISE PASCAL

Though faith may act more easily when it has some help from sense, yet it acts most nobly when it acts in opposition to sense. Then it is pure faith when it stands upon its own legs – the power and Word of God.

THOMAS BOSTON

A grace mysterious in its commencement as in its consummation, and of which merely intellectual faith and a merely logical assurance of salvation is only the counterfeit.

ALEXANDRE VINET

Faith means a Spirit-given trust in the divine mercy and on a personal Saviour, as opposed to man's native self-reliance! It is saving only as it is receptive of Christ's finished work . . . A God-given reliance on an all-sufficient Mediator.

GEORGE SMEATON

Faith enables us to measure the world at its real value.

HENRY LIDDON

Faith consists of three things: knowledge, assent, confidence. These mean knowledge of the testimony, certainty of the things revealed, persuasion that this concerns me personally.

Without Scripture, faith is an aimless gazing; without faith Scripture is a closed book . . . Faith and Scripture belong together.

Faith is not the working of a faculty inherent in the natural man . . . but a disposition, mode of action, implanted by the Holy Spirit in the consciousness and will of the regenerate person.

ABRAHAM KUYPER

Faith in principles is not a question of majorities. 'Monks are not reasons.'

AUGUSTE LECERF

Faith is a psychological, moral and spiritual impossibility apart from an efficacious drawing which is of the nature of a gift from the Father.

JOHN MURRAY

Faith . . . is not merely rational assent, but a movement of the whole nature by the direct action of the Holy Spirit.

G. W. BROMILEY

FAMILY

Plato's *Republic* only regarded the prosperity of the Commonwealth. The value of the individual soul, the sanctity of the family life, were mysteries to him.

ADOLPH SAPHIR

[In the second and third centuries] the gospel penetrated successively the regions of domestic life, of speculation, of government.

BROOKE FOSS WESCOTT

Education is not primarily the concern of the school, or even of the State, but of the family.

EMIL BRUNNER

Within your own houses, I say, in some cases you are bishops and kings, your wife, children, servants and family are your bishopric and charge; of you it shall be required how carefully and diligently you have always instructed them in God's true knowledge . . . Make them partakers in reading, exhorting and in making common prayers in every house, once a day at least.

JOHN KNOX,
Letter from Geneva to Scotland

All the families of the pious should be regulated in such a manner as to be so many little churches.

[*On Psalm 127:3*] The meaning is that children are not the fruit of chance, but that God, as it seems good to him, distributes to every man his share of them.

JOHN CALVIN

I saw reason to bless the Lord that I had been made the father of six children, now in the grave, and that were with me but a very short time; but none of them lost; I will see them all at the resurrection.

THOMAS BOSTON

The family is the primary institution of God for killing the natural self-seeking of the individual.

JAMES CANDLISH

Modern society has committed a serious mistake by substituting the school for the familial training.

ALEXIS CARRELL

FANATICS/FANATICISM

Well does Chrysostom admonish us to reject all, who, under the pretence of the Spirit, lead us away from the simple doctrine of the gospel – the Spirit having promised not to reveal new doctrine, but to impress the truth of the gospel on our minds.

Frantic men require inspirations and revelations from heaven, and condemn the ministers of God by whose hand they ought to be governed.

When they extravagantly boast of the Spirit, the tendency certainly is to sink and bury the Word of God.

The fanaticism which discards the Scriptures under the pretence of resorting to immediate revelations is subversive of every principle of piety.

'The Word' must not be separated from 'the Spirit', as the fanatics imagine, who, despising the Word, glory in the name of the Spirit . . . It is the spirit of Satan that is separated from the Word, to which the Spirit of God is continually joined.

JOHN CALVIN

We are left unto the Word alone for the trial of any who pretend unto extraordinary gifts.

JOHN OWEN

FEAR OF GOD

Such as are edified to fear and obey God are men of right understanding.

[On Psalm 68:35] If you are not yet filled with awe and reverence, fear and trembling, do not think you know God . . . This fear is the highest form of worship of God.

I understand fear in general to mean the feeling of piety which is produced in us by the knowledge of the power, equity and mercy of God.

How shall we fear God unless we know that all our welfare lies in Him?

He walks in darkness who is not ruled by the fear of God.

All those who do not draw nigh to God with all their heart, are compelled to stand before the judgment seat of man.

God includes *faith* in the word *fear*. What is the cause that men are in a continual fear, but that they cannot commend their life into the hand of God?

The fear which God requires is matched with hearty love.

Under this 'fear of God' is comprehended all religion.

JOHN CALVIN

He that fears God loveth His Word, and liveth unto the same.

HUGH LATIMER

The fear of God turns other fears out of doors.

Right fear proceeds from faith; false fear from doubt.

ROBERT LEIGHTON

He who examines it is startled to find that the phrase, 'the fear of the Lord', is woven into the whole web of Revelation from Genesis to the Apocalypse.

All great religious awakenings begin in the dawning of the august and terrible aspects of the Deity upon the popular mind, and they reach their height and happy consummation, in that love and faith for which the antecedent fear has been the preparation.

WILLIAM G.T. SHEDD

FEARS

Guilty consciences are so disturbed by blind and unreasonable fears, that they become their own tormentors.

Of little dwarfs we make giants.

The person who will be afraid of a mortal creature, and would be loath to offend him, will anger God boldly and without remorse of conscience.

Faith in God clears the mind and dispels carnal fears.

ROBERT LEIGHTON

FLATTERY

Enemies sometimes use praises like prefaces that they may the more freely calumniate afterwards.

Men immoderately extol those of their own, and depress those of the opposite party.

Those who praise or dispraise commonly have their own views in it, and speak not their real sentiments.

JOHN CALVIN

FREE WILL[1]

Free will [is] putting conversion in the power of man.

Free will assents to God calling and exciting it . . . God acts within, holds our hearts, moves our hearts, and draws us by the inclinations He has produced in us.

JOHN CALVIN

[*Sovereignty and free-will*]. The true object is gained not by magnifying natural ability, and shutting men up to will, but by exhibiting the two sides of the incomprehensible mystery. They are both true; and all that theology effects is to conserve the mystery.

GEORGE SMEATON

[1] See also RESPONSIBILITY

FRIENDSHIP

You cannot be my friend unless you desire my good.

AUGUSTINE

Youth is the time for forming friendships. Later years, when peculiarities become settled and confirmed, make us more conscious of difference than of affinity in others.

CHRISTOPH LUTHARDT

The worst solitude is to want friends.

The sun has more admirers rising than setting.

FRANCIS BACON

It is the destiny of old men to lose their most devoted friends.

ROBERT FLINT

God, working ever on a social plan,
By various ties attaches man
    to man.

WILLIAM COWPER

THE FUTURE

Looking to the Risen Christ we Christians live in the future, even more than in the present: it is part of our nature to do so.

HENRY LIDDON

GENTLENESS

He who would be a good teacher must be gentle and leave some means to draw those who come to him, that he may win them.

God would fain draw us to Him by gentleness.

Often the immoderate heat of the pastors in going about matters does no less hurt than their sluggishness.

JOHN CALVIN

GIFTS

Perseverance [is] the great gift of God, whereby His other gifts are preserved.

AUGUSTINE

All the gifts and power that men seem to possess are in the hand of God, so that He can, at any instant, deprive them of the wisdom which He has given them.

God has always deliberately distributed the gifts of his Spirit in limited measure to those whom He has truly established as doctors in His church.

Many foolishly imagine that Christ taught only so as to lay down the first lessons, and then to send the disciples to a higher school . . . They substitute the Spirit in his place.

It is notorious that the gifts of the Spirit, which were then given by the laying on of hands, some time after ceased to be conferred.

All the gifts God gives us are matched with as many infirmities.

The gift of tongues and other such gifts are ceased long ago in the church.

All prophets and ministers of God ought to watch against being covetous of gifts.

Many men excel oftentimes in the gifts of the Spirit who have an unclean heart.

There is something of the divine nature in the least grace that is not in the most glorious gifts.

The Corinthians abused the gifts of God for ostentation and show . . . Would to God there were no Corinth in our times!

Gifts of themselves have not this power . . . They change not the heart, they renew not the mind, they transform not the soul into the image of God.

JOHN CALVIN

Great grace and small gifts are better than great gifts and no grace.

JOHN BUNYAN

The Holy Spirit gives out His gifts and powers unto men in many parts, not all to one, not all in one way, but some to one, some to another, some at one time, some at another, and that in great variety.

JOHN OWEN

The ordinary influence of the Spirit of God, working the grace of charity in the heart, is a more excellent blessing than any of the extraordinary gifts.

All the *charismata* are only means of grace, but charity or divine love is grace itself.

JONATHAN EDWARDS

Some of the gifts were designed for the first age of the Church. They have ceased . . . We have no workers of miracles, no speakers with tongues.

CHARLES HODGE

GLORY FOR GOD ALONE

There ought to be moderation in our respect for God's prophets . . . He alone may be exalted.

We must speak of the efficacy of the ministry in such a manner that the entire praise of the work may be reserved for God alone.

JOHN CALVIN

God can do wonders with little noise.

THOMAS BOSTON

GOD

The will of God is never defeated, though much is done that is contrary to His will . . . Even what is done in opposition to His will does not defeat His will.

AUGUSTINE

Whatever we think and whatever we say of Him should savour of His excellence, correspond to the sacred sublimity of His Name and tend to the exaltation of His magnificence.

We must always remind ourselves of this word, 'God must do it.'

When men seek to comprehend the power of God, it is like a fly attempting to devour all the mountains.

God, by His secret inspiration, moves forms, governs and draws men's hearts, so that even by the wicked – He executes whatever He has decreed.

Teachers [that is, ministers] cannot firmly execute their office except they have the majesty of God before their eyes.

It is good reason that all creatures should suffer themselves to be ruled by Him, and not take liberty to rule themselves.

JOHN CALVIN

My faith hath no bed to sleep upon but omnipotency.

SAMUEL RUTHERFORD

The incomprehensible, infinite and most perfect holiness or purity of God is the cause why He hates and detests all sin.

JOHN OWEN

If the full-orbed idea [of God] be so mutilated that nothing but the feeling of love is allowed to enter into the nature of God, the mind softens and melts away into moral imbecility.

WILLIAM G. T. SHEDD

GOOD WORKS

The merit of works ceases when righteousness is sought by faith.

Faith, which is given by God's grace to the ungodly, and by which they are justified, is the substance, foundation, fountain, source, chief and firstborn of all spiritual graces, gifts, virtues, merits and works.

MARTIN LUTHER

We must first be made good, before we can be good.

God will reward good works *in* everlasting life, but not *with* everlasting life.

HUGH LATIMER

Not only our persons, but even our works are justified by faith alone.

JOHN CALVIN

That which is the true saint's super-structure is the hypocrite's foundation.

JONATHAN EDWARDS

Though we have no works to perform in order to be justified, we have everything to do in order to manifest our gratitude and love (*Rom.*3:31).

CHARLES HODGE

Good works are the ripe fruit of the tree which the Lord has planted in sanctification . . . Except the breath of the Lord blow through the garden of the soul, not a leaf can stir.

ABRAHAM KUYPER

GROWING OLD

Youth knows not, and age cannot.

Ought we not to be greatly ashamed if we do not store up God's Word in old age?

The chief part of a good old age consists in a good conscience and in a serene and tranquil mind.

The most part of men become more fools in their age than they were in their youth.

The guilt of the old is always the heaviest.

JOHN CALVIN

I try daily to learn something new, and thus to prevent my old age from becoming listless and inert.

ANDREW MELVILLE

A graceless old age is a lamentable sight.

ROBERT LEIGHTON

A steady spiritual view of the glory of Christ by faith, will give a gracious revival from inward decays, and fresh springs of grace, even in the latter days.

JOHN OWEN

Few men grow zealous for peace till they grow old.

RICHARD BAXTER

Remember it is a remark of old and experienced men that very few men, and very few ministers, keep up to the end the edge that was on their spirits at the first.

ANDREW BONAR

My voice fails, some of my people, especially the younger part, going elsewhere; my class melts away; some very mortifying case of ingratitude . . . my interest with brethren manifestly declines.

ANDREW BONAR

Age rubs down a good deal the controversial spirit of a man.

JOHN DUNCAN

We are inexorably separated by age from one another. A mother never succeeds in being a sister to her daughter. It is impossible for children to understand their parents, still less their grandparents.

ALEXIS CARRELL

GUIDANCE

Walk in the light of faith within the limits of God's Word.

We must take God for our Guide and Leader all our lives.

Let us not attempt anything, in all our whole life, except we know it be acceptable to our God.

He will attend to our welfare . . . Seeing we are His children there is no cause to doubt.

God will not suffer us to err unless we do it wittingly.

Sometimes He preserves us by His power that we fall not at all; and sometimes He suffers us to fall to lift us up afterwards.

When there is no way out, nor clear path, at that point God will faithfully guide us by our Lord Jesus Christ . . . insofar as we allow ourselves to be taught by him.

JOHN CALVIN

Ruth Bell felt called to West China, Billy Graham to evangelism. Their engagement was imperilled. Billy asked, 'Do you think God has brought us together?' Ruth admitted God had. Billy went on, 'The Bible teaches the husband is the head of his wife. The Lord leads and you follow.' Ruth agreed in faith.

JOHN POLLOCK on the Grahams

HAPPINESS

The happy life is to rejoice in God and for God.

AUGUSTINE

Happy is the sadness of the faithful, which has such joy with it, and unhappy is the joy of unbelievers, which has such sadness with it.

MARTIN LUTHER

They who desire to be happy in the world renounce heaven.

JOHN CALVIN

The highest happiness consists in holiness. This will make a man happy without anything else. But no other enjoyments or privileges whatsoever will make a man happy without this.

JONATHAN EDWARDS

I never was acquainted with rational happiness till my attention was turned to religion. My former merriment was like the crackling of thorns under a pot.

JAMES HALDANE

Happiness depends on one's being exactly fitted for the nature of one's work.

ALEXIS CARRELL

HEALTH

To how many health is an injury!

AUGUSTINE

Consider always what is fit and profitable for our health . . . that we use not too great austereness, for God will not have men to kill themselves.

All the promises contained in Holy Scripture are, as it were, so many testimonies of the fatherly love of our God, showing Himself to have a care of our health and welfare.

JOHN CALVIN

I am never better than when I am on the full stretch for God.

GEORGE WHITEFIELD

The sound body lives in silence. We do not hear, we do not feel its working.

ALEXIS CARRELL

THE HEART

There is not one of us but makes a den of thieves of his own heart.

[This knowledge and assent] which we give to the Divine Word is from the heart rather than the head, and from the affections rather than the understanding.

JOHN CALVIN

Where light leaves the affections behind, it ends in formality or atheism; and where affections out-run light, they sink into a bog of superstition, doting on images and pictures and the like.

JOHN OWEN

HEAVEN

There is a City of God, and its Founder has inspired us with a love which makes us covet its citizenship.

There we shall rest and see, see and love, love and praise. This is what shall be in the end without end.

AUGUSTINE

Since Christ entered in our nature, and, as it were, in our names . . . we not only hope for heaven, but already possess it in our Head.

JOHN CALVIN

Heaven is principally represented to us as the place of the residence and glory of Jesus Christ in the administration of His office.

JOHN OWEN

If contentment were here heaven were not heaven.

SAMUEL RUTHERFORD

Heaven is a state in which the Holy Spirit shall be more perfectly and abundantly given to the Church than He is now on earth. But the way it shall be given will be in that great fruit of love, the Spirit, holy and divine, in the hearts of the blessed inhabitants of that world.

JONATHAN EDWARDS

HELL

A deep-rooted infidelity lurks in men's minds on the subject of hell.

HELL
(Continued)

I see it oozing out in the utter apathy of some; they eat, and drink, and sleep, as if there were no wrath to come. I see it creeping forth in the coldness of others about their neighbour's souls: they show little anxiety to pluck brands from the fire. I desire to denounce such infidelity with all my might.

J. C. Ryle

Sir, you often told me of Christ and salvation: why did you not oftener remind me of hell and danger?

A Hearer, to John Newton

All hell should be ringing with the praises of penal justice — it is duty.

John Duncan

The lost will eternally suffer in the satisfaction of justice. But they will never satisfy it. Christ satisfied justice (*Isa.*53:6).

John Murray

HOLY SCRIPTURE [1]

Whenever we take the sacred books in our hands, the blood of Christ ought to occur to our minds, as if the whole of its sacred instruction were written therewith.

We must come to this point that our faith be grounded on the Word

[1] See also The Bible

of God, and that the Holy Scripture be all our wisdom.

God wishes that the reverence which He exacts from us be given to His own Word.

As the hearts of men are attracted to Jesus Christ, their minds are filled with reverence and love for the Scriptures.

John Calvin

The Scriptures spring out of God, and flow into Christ, and were given to lead us to Christ.

William Tyndale

The deniers of Christianity in the early ages granted, with hardly an exception, the genuineness of the Christian documents, while these in the 18th century were largely disputed or denied.

John Cairns

The Bible as it stands is a miracle! Only on the supposition of one authorship behind the human composition; of one Spirit inspiring many writers, is this possible.

J. Elder Cumming

HOLY SCRIPTURE – THE SPIRIT'S TESTIMONY

They who have been inwardly taught by the Spirit, feel an entire acquiescence in the Scripture, and that it is self-authenticated.

The testimony of the Holy Spirit means that the necessity of external proofs that the Scriptures are the Word of God is superseded.

God does not bestow the Spirit on His people in order to set aside the use of His Word, but rather to render it fruitful.

The true conviction which believers have of the word of God, of their own salvation, and of religion in general, does not spring from the judgment of the flesh, or from human and philosophical arguments, but from the sealing of the Spirit, who imparts to their conscience such certainty as to remove all doubt.

The faithful, inwardly illuminated by the Holy Spirit, acknowledge nothing but what God says in His Word.

The same Spirit who made Moses and the prophets certain of their calling, now also testifies to our hearts, that He has employed them as his servants to instruct.

JOHN CALVIN

We are completely and utterly incapable of understanding Scripture. We must first receive from God the intelligence for this, and God gives us this when we turn to him, by his Spirit.

W. NIESEL

The testimony of the Holy Spirit is that subjective action of the Holy Spirit upon the heart, by virtue of which it is opened for the perfection and reception of the objective revelation of God.

B. B. WARFIELD

God's elect obtain a firm assurance concerning the Word of God that nothing can shake . . . He supports the conviction continually.

ABRAHAM KUYPER

The truth of God, sealed by the Holy Spirit on our hearts, despises and defies all that is in the world . . . this single Witness powerfully drives away, scatters, and overturns all that the world rears up to obscure or crush the truth of God.

The veil which is spread over the Scriptures for the Jews is also there for false Christians, and for all who do not hate themselves.

BLAISE PASCAL

Apart from the testimony of the Spirit . . . there is no true vital faith in the Word of God.

ADOLPH SAPHIR

He alone who is taught by the Spirit of God can know the true use and value of Holy Scripture.

SAMUEL P. TREGELLES

HOLY SCRIPTURE – TESTIMONIES OF BELIEVERS

Wonderful is the depth of Thy oracles, whose surface is before us, inviting the little ones; and yet wonderful is the depth, O my God, wonderful is the depth. It is awe to look into it; an awe of honour, and a tremor of love.

AUGUSTINE

We bear such reverence to God's Word as we acknowledge it to be the most precious treasure we have.

JOHN CALVIN

He that fears God loves His Word, and lives unto the same.

HUGH LATIMER

I am a Christian . . . I die testifying against all who make not the Scriptures, which are the Word of God, their rule.

DONALD CARGILL

I die, adhering to the Scriptures of the Old and New Testaments as the undoubted Word of God.

JOHN NISBET

The Scottish Covenanting preacher, Alexander Peden, speaks of an old widow in Clydesdale. She was asked how she did in this evil time. 'I do very well,' says she. 'I get more good of one verse of the Bible now than I did of it all lang syne. He hath cast me the keys of the pantry door, and bidden me take my fill.'

ALEXANDER SMELLIE

I daily received fresh life, light and power from above . . . more true knowledge from reading the Book of God in one month than I could ever have acquired from all the writings of men.

GEORGE WHITEFIELD

You will notice that those who make most of the Word of God make most progress in the divine life.

HORATIUS BONAR

Our gracious King; we present you with this Book, the most valuable thing that this world affords. Here is wisdom; this is the Royal Law; these are the lively oracles of God.

WORDS USED AT THE CORONATION OF BRITISH SOVEREIGNS

Since I have learned to read the Bible in this way . . . it becomes more marvellous to me every day. You will not believe how glad one is to find one's way back to these elementary things after wandering on a lot of theological side-paths.

DIETRICH BONHOEFFER

HOLY SCRIPTURE – DIFFICULTIES IN

The Holy Spirit has, with admirable wisdom, and care for our welfare, so arranged the Holy Scriptures as by the plainer passages to satisfy our hunger, and by the more obscure to stimulate our appetite. For almost nothing is dug out of these obscure passages which may not be found set forth in the plainest language elsewhere.

Christ gives us what is plain for food; what is more obscure for exercise.

AUGUSTINE

We are permitted to pour into God's bosom the difficulties which torment us, in order that He may loosen the knots we cannot untie.

God does not in every way untie all the knots by which we are entangled.

Every truth that is preached of Christ is quite paradoxical to human judgments.

Where the Lord closes his holy mouth let us also stop our minds from going on further.

JOHN CALVIN

Where Scriptures, at first sight, do contradict one another, we must, by a serious consideration of them, labour to discover their harmony. But if we should not be able to reconcile them, we ought not to pronounce them irreconcilable, but rather attribute a deficiency to our own understanding.

JOHN BROWN of Haddington

Faith in Christ's Person is the final answer to all difficulties and objections.

ALFRED EDERSHEIM

THE HOLY SPIRIT

The question why the Holy Spirit is not begotten, and how He proceeds from the Father and the Son, will only be answered when we are in bliss.

The Lord Jesus Christ Himself not only gave the Holy Spirit as God, but also received Him as man (*Luke* 2:52;4:1). How great a God is He who gives God!

We have now received 'the earnest'(*2 Cor.*1:22) . . . His fullness is reserved for us till another life.

AUGUSTINE

The gift of the Spirit was a fruit of the resurrection of Christ.

The principal end of the Holy Spirit's sending was to glorify the Son.

We are partakers of the Holy Spirit according to the intercourse we maintain with Christ; the Spirit will be found nowhere but in Christ.

Nothing is bestowed on us by the Spirit apart from Christ, but He takes it from Christ that He may communicate it to us ...The Spirit enriches us with no other than the riches of Christ, that He may display His glory in all things.

JOHN CALVIN

THE HOLY SPIRIT
(CONTINUED)

If we will have God to continue the grace of the Holy Spirit . . . we must learn to exalt and magnify him as he deserves, and to acknowledge that there is not one drop of good understanding in us till God has put it into us.

The Holy Spirit is the bond by which Christ efficaciously unites us to Himself.

The Holy Spirit is like a living and continually flowing fountain in believers . . . Everyone partakes of the gifts and graces of the Spirit according to his faith.

God raised up men to be as instruments and working tools of His Holy Spirit.

None are called to obtain the riches of the Spirit, but those who burn with desire for them.

JOHN CALVIN

The most powerful means that ever was ordained for our good will be dead and heartless if He be not there by His Spirit.

RICHARD SIBBES

As the work of the Son is not His own work, but rather the 'work of the Father who sent Him', and in whose name He performed it, so the work of the Spirit is not His own work, but rather the work of the Son, by whom He is sent, and in whose name he does accomplish it. The Holy Spirit supplies the bodily absence of Christ; hence He is 'the vicar of Christ' (as some ancients call Him).

JOHN OWEN

The graces and influences of the Holy Spirit give legs, strength and vigour to the inner man to run, as wind does a ship.

JAMES DURHAM

The Holy Spirit is for ever to be communicated to the saints in the grace of charity, or divine love.

JONATHAN EDWARDS

Without a full testimony to the divine personality and agency of the Holy Spirit no blessing can be expected on the ministrations of any church.

The isolation of the Spirit's work from the cross and crown of the Redeemer is always of doubtful tendency . . . Much loose thinking and unsound doctrine are always disseminated when the Spirit's work within is made to eclipse or overshadow the Redeemer's finished work without.

GEORGE SMEATON

What air is to a man's physical nature, the Holy Spirit is to man's spiritual nature. Without air there is death in our bodies; without the Holy Spirit there is death in our souls.

Except the breath of the Lord blow through the garden of the soul, not a leaf can stir.

ABRAHAM KUYPER

The office of the Holy Spirit is to convey Christ's nature and to interpret his teaching to Christians.

HENRY LIDDON

The Holy Spirit not only originates faith, but increases it by degrees, till He conducts us by it all the way to the heavenly kingdom.

OSCAR CULLMANN

THE SPIRIT'S SEALING AND ILLUMINATING

The Holy Spirit can fill your heart with a single word.

MARTIN LUTHER

Till the Holy Spirit has become our instructor, all that we know is folly and ignorance.

The testimony of the Spirit is superior to all reason . . . The word will never gain credit in the hearts of men till it be confirmed by the internal testimony of the Spirit.

It is not sufficient for us to be imbued once with the illumination of the Holy Spirit, unless God works in us daily.

The Holy Spirit may be justly called the key with which the treasures of the kingdom of heaven are un-

locked to us; and His illumination constitutes our mental eyes to behold them.

JOHN CALVIN

HOPE

We must not judge of things at the first sight . . . but hope must go before us and be as a lamp to show us the way . . . And what is the oil of this lamp? . . . Sticking to God's promises.

There would be no occasion for exercising hope were our salvation complete.

When hope animates us, there is a vigour in the whole body.

It behoves us to ask . . . that He would increase our hope when it is small; awaken it when it is dormant; confirm it when it is wavering; strengthen it when it is weak; and raise it up when it is overthrown.

JOHN CALVIN

HUMILITY

We must boast in nothing, since nothing is our own.

CYPRIAN, quoted by Augustine

Jesus washes not the disciples hands, but their feet . . . As the Master of humility.

Lest man should disdain to imitate a humble man, God humbled

HUMILITY
(CONTINUED)

Himself so that the pride of the human race might not disdain to walk in the footsteps of God.

There is something in humility which, strangely enough, exalts the heart, and something in pride which debases it.

AUGUSTINE

Humility is the foundation of our philosophy.

JOHN CHRYSOSTOM

Humility is the only response we should have towards a God who has given everything for our sake.

[*Psalm 119:131*] O most beautiful humility . . . He preferred to be taught rather than to teach.

Faith is founded on humility for it has for its guide and teacher the Holy Spirit.

He that is highest of all, if he pass not others in humbleness, it is certain that he shall daily cast himself headlong into destruction and confusion.

True faith always expresses itself by humility. It makes a man willing to count himself nothing, while attributing all praise to God.

God always kept his prophets humble . . . They would recognize that they were not angels.

Humility . . . the mother of moderation . . . depends on a right estimate of God's gifts and our own infirmities.

JOHN CALVIN

You have borne patiently with my vehemence, which was sometimes carried to excess . . . I again entreat you to pardon my infirmities which I acknowledge and confess before God and His angels, and before you, my much respected Lords.

JOHN CALVIN, at his death, to the City Fathers of Geneva.

Few speak humbly of humility.

BLAISE PASCAL

Pray much for the spirit of humility, the Spirit of Christ, for that it is.

The humblest Christian is the strongest.

ROBERT LEIGHTON

A sense of the loveliness of God is peculiarly that discovery of God that works humility.

The more excellent anything is the more will be the counterfeits of it. There are perhaps no graces which have more counterfeits than love and humility.

JONATHAN EDWARDS

God give me a deep humility, a well guided zeal, a burning love, a single eye, and then let men or devils do their worst.

GEORGE WHITEFIELD

Sir, you do not preach enough about humility; that's my forte.

A WOMAN, to ALEXANDER MOODY STUART

I would rather have the smallest portion of humility and love than the knowledge of an archangel.

HENRY MARTYN

IMPUTATION

In its principal meaning of 'reckoning to the account of another' it is found in: 1. The imputation of Adam's sin to man (*Rom*. 5;12–21). 2. The imputation of the sin of man to Christ (*Isa*. 53:4–6). 3. The imputation of the righteousness of God to the believer (*Rom*.3:22; 5:17–19).

BAKER'S DICTIONARY OF THEOLOGY

INTELLECT

Almost all of us have received the word about God through faith, without having a secondary training in Greek philosophy, some of us without elementary education.

CLEMENT OF ALEXANDRIA

Clever people who neglect their minds and are impious can lose their gift . . . and diligent and pious people who are of a slower under-

standing can nevertheless reach understanding.

Intelligence is the gift of God.

AUGUSTINE

Faith, far from arresting the play of thought, stimulates it.

ANSELM

The manifold agility of the soul, which enables it to take a survey of heaven and earth; to join the past and the present; to retain the memory of things heard long ago; to conceive of whatever it chooses by the help of imagination; its ingenuity also in the invention of such admirable arts – are certain proof of the divinity in men.

Human sagacity is here [in matters of faith] so completely lost that the first step to improvement in the divine school, is to forsake it.

If we excel in understanding, we are not to abuse this singular gift of God.

The mind of man is God's true image.

Natural perspicacity is a gift of God, and the liberal arts, and all the sciences by which wisdom is acquired, are gifts of God . . . They must occupy the place of handmaid, not of mistress.

JOHN CALVIN

INTELLECT
(CONTINUED)

Man's mind has shown itself most excellent in all branches of knowledge, except in the chief, to know how to come to Him.

No man . . . can arrive at faith by his own sagacity; all are blind until they are illuminated by the Spirit of God.

JOHN CALVIN

The mind of man hath so large room to receive good things that nothing indeed can fully fill it but God only.

JOHN BRADFORD

God alone can put [divine truths] into the soul . . . He chooses that they should pass from the heart into the understanding, and not from the understanding into the heart, in order to humble that proud faculty of reason.

BLAISE PASCAL

That knowledge which is the first part of the renewed image of God is . . . a beam of God's own, issuing from Himself, both enlightening and enlivening the whole soul; it gains the affection and stirs to action . . . it acts and increases by acting.

ROBERT LEIGHTON

This strengthening of the mind by saving illumination is the most eminent act of our sanctification.

JOHN OWEN

The Spirit . . . sets the reason free to do justice to the evidence before it.

HENRY LIDDON

Intellectual torpor is a form of death.

JOHN DUNCAN

I once put the question to Dr Robert Laws of Livingstonia, 'What do your people in Nyasaland make of a great part of the New Testament, say the Epistles to the Romans or Ephesians? Can they understand it?' 'Well,' was the answer, 'I have generally found that where there has been a religious awakening in any man or people, a very remarkable intellectual awakening goes along with it.'

W. T. CAIRUS

Intelligence is almost useless to those who possess nothing else. The pure intellectual is an incomplete human being.

ALEXIS CARRELL

When man becomes a believer, powers are released which he did not know he possessed before. Through faith, therefore, human beings with a very modest outfit of intellectual powers often develop amazingly, reaching an extraordinary degree of mental independence and freedom of spirit, wisdom and clearness, compared with which a far greater intellectual ability looks meagre.

EMIL BRUNNER

Apollos was a D.Litt, but he had to be instructed by two tent makers.

HERBERT MINN

INTERCESSION [1]

Our commending one another to God (in our prayers and supplications) is the chief duty of love.

Often God spares us because there are some who make intercession for us.

JOHN CALVIN

The great Advocate pleadeth hard for you; be upon the Advocate's side, O poor feared client of Christ.

SAMUEL RUTHERFORD

Intercessory prayer – the most conspicuous instance of mutual support in the communion of saints.

HENRY SWETE

JESTING

I hate that preaching which tendeth to make the hearers laugh. You cannot break men's hearts by jesting with them.

RICHARD BAXTER

JESUS CHRIST – GOD

The Father is greater than the form of a servant, to whom, in the form of God, the Son is equal.

AUGUSTINE

[1] See also PRAYER

Christ, considered in Himself, is called God; but with relation to the Father, He is called the Son.

JOHN CALVIN

Those who, denying that [divine] nature in Christ, do yet pretend to worship Him, with divine and religious adoration, do but worship a golden calf of their own setting-up.

JOHN OWEN

Adam's guilt is imputed to his posterity. But Christ is not a descendant of Adam. He existed before Adam . . . His *ego* is that of the Person of the Son of God.

ABRAHAM KUYPER

The martyrs of the primitive Church died in a great number of cases expressly for the dogma of Christ's Divinity.

[His] most startling revelation was Himself.

To charge Christ with error is to deny that He is God.

HENRY LIDDON

The Greek word *Lord* (*ton Kurion*) was the Septuagint equivalent of the Hebrew Yahweh (Jehovah).

J. N. D. KELLY

JESUS CHRIST – MAN

According to the form of God, all things were made by Him (*John1*:3); according to the form of

JESUS CHRIST – MAN
(CONTINUED)

a servant, He was Himself made of a woman, made under the law (*Gal*.4:4).

Lord of Mary and Son of Mary . . . He created her of whom, as man, He was to be created.

AUGUSTINE

Christ voluntarily took on Him all that is inseparable from human nature.

Jesus Christ, the Lord of glory, abased Himself so low as to become the servant of servants.

JOHN CALVIN

His human nature had no distinct personality nor any self-directing principle apart from the personal union.

The human nature of Christ, in His divine Person, and together with it, is the chief object of all divine adoration and worship.

The body of Christ, being formed pure and exact by the Holy Ghost, there was no disposition or tendency in His constitution to the least deviation from perfect holiness in any kind.

As to our bodily diseases and distempers, which personally adhere unto us, upon the disorder and vice of our constitutions, He was absolutely free from them.

It is not enough that He has taken our nature to be His, unless He gives us also His nature to be ours.

The human nature [in Christ] was not the residential subject of omnisciency. He speaks of Himself [in *Mark* 13:32] with respect unto His human nature only . . . the human nature, therefore, however inconceivably advanced, is not the subject of infinite, essentially divine properties.

JOHN OWEN

The mystery of the incarnation lies in the apparent contradiction of Christ's union with our fallen nature, which, on the one hand, is so intimate as to make Him susceptible to its temptations, while, on the other hand, He is completely cut off from all fellowship with its sin . . . He is made sin, but never a sinner.

His self-emptying was not a single loss or bereavement, but a growing poorer and poorer, until at last nothing was left Him but a piece of ground where he could weep and a cross whereon He could die.

ABRAHAM KUYPER

When Jesus Christ ceases to be perfect God He ceases to be perfect man . . . To let Christ be diminished is to lose Him.

ALEXANDRE VINET

The doctrine of the Two Natures is only another way of stating the doctrine of the Incarnation; and the doctrine of the Incarnation is the hinge on which the Christian system turns.

Nothing that is human is alien to Him except sin. He never ascribes imperfection to Himself and never betrays consciousness of sin.

B. B. WARFIELD

JESUS CHRIST – TO BE KNOWN

When Christ is not known it is impossible to have any understanding in Scripture.

To know Him is to know and have everything.

MARTIN LUTHER

[Christ] appears to us daily by His gospel. Let us open the eyes of our faith, and we shall see how He shows Himself to us.

The only way of retaining, as well as restoring true doctrine [is] to place Christ before the view, such as He is, with all His blessings, that His excellence may be perceived.

Our Lord Jesus Christ will be sufficient light for us, both in life and death.

He who does not perceive Christ to be God is blind amidst the brightness of noonday.

JOHN CALVIN

The beholding of Christ is the most blessed means of exciting all our graces, spiritualizing all our affections, and transforming our minds into His likeness.

[On the mode of our transformation, as in 2 Cor. 3:18] Let that glory be rightly stated – the glory of His Person, His office, His condescension, exaltation and love and grace; let faith be fixed in a view and contemplation of it, mix itself with it, as represented in the glass of the gospel, meditate upon it, embrace it – and virtue will proceed from Christ, communicating spiritual, supernatural refreshment and joy to our souls.

So much as we know of Christ, His sufferings, and His glory, so much do we understand of the Scripture, and no more.

JOHN OWEN

Above all knowledge, know Christ.

JOHN WESLEY

The incarnate Son of God is the focal point of divine revelation.

JOHN MURRAY

JESUS CHRIST – HIS VIRGIN BIRTH

No one can say, without violation of the Christian faith, that *perhaps* Christ was born of a virgin.

AUGUSTINE

JESUS CHRIST –
HIS VIRGIN BIRTH
(Continued)

The same overshadowing power which formed His human nature reforms ours . . . He who was born for us upon His incarnation, is born within us upon our regeneration.

John Pearson, quoting Jerome

The conception of the Mediator . . . is not the conception of a human person but of a human nature.

Abraham Kuyper

As early as St Ignatius (died c.107 AD) the Virgin Birth figured in summaries of the *kerygma* [preaching], and the fathers fastened on Isaiah 7:14ff. as its prophetic anticipation.

J. N. D. Kelly

JESUS CHRIST –
OBEDIENCE
AND DEATH

To be forsaken by the Father was death to the Son. The Son both dies at the Father's hand, and is raised by the Father, according to the Scriptures.

Tertullian

The whole life of our Lord Jesus Christ has become our ransom, for the obedience which He yielded in this world to God His Father was to make amends for Adam's offence and for all the iniquities for which we are in debt.

The obedience which Jesus Christ has yielded to God, His Father, is set over unto us as if we ourselves had fulfilled the whole law.

He was obedient for us . . . our heavenly Father admits us as if we brought perfect obedience with us. The obedience which He yielded unto His Father is our righteousness.

He bore in His soul the tortures of condemned and ruined man.

He endured the pains of hell for a time to free and acquit me.

The efficacy of His sacrifice is eternal – and the benefit of it is received by us every day.

The species of death which Christ suffered is fraught with a peculiar mystery. The cross was accursed, not only in the opinion of men, but by the decree of the divine law.

John Calvin

He suffered not as God, but He suffered who was God.

John Owen

I am no preacher; let this hint suffice –
The cross, once seen, is death to every vice;
Else he who hung there suffered all His pain,
Bled, groaned, and agonized, and died in vain.

William Cowper

It is in the soul of Jesus that we must seek for the true passion of the God-man. And what human soul could ever have suffered what He did?

ALEXANDRE VINET

Every event of His life was a part of His payment of the penalty of sin, and every event of His life was a part of that glorious keeping of the law of God by which He earned for His people the reward of eternal life. The two aspects of His work are inextricably intertwined . . . Together they constitute the wonderful, full salvation which was wrought for us by Christ our Redeemer.

J. GRESHAM MACHEN

God's justice is met by the active and passive obedience of Christ, or by a subjection to the law in its precept as well as in its penalty.

GEORGE SMEATON

It would be preposterous that God would leave us in any uncertainty as to what His gospel is, or should send us good tidings whose meaning we were unable clearly to grasp. On the contrary the Gospel is fully explained in the Bible, and its explanation can be summed up in one word 'substitution'.

THOMAS MILLER

The obedience of Christ is that which procured salvation in broadest compass.

JOHN MURRAY

JESUS CHRIST – RISEN AND LIVING

So the flesh rises again, in its entirety, in its identity, in its integrity.

TERTULLIAN

The resurrection . . . the chief point of the Gospel.

The resurrection, the closing scene of our redemption. For the lively assurance of our reconciliation with God arises from Christ having come from hell as the conqueror of death.

The odour of His resurrection has now sufficient efficacy, without spikenard, and costly ointments, to quicken the whole world.

The resurrection of Christ, by its quickening vigour, penetrated every sepulchre.

The resurrection of Christ is the commencement of His reign.

Christ lives for us, not for Himself . . . nor has Christ anything which may not be applied to our benefit.

If the resurrection is overthrown the dominion of sin is set up anew.

All ministers of the Word ought to be exceeding careful that the glory of the resurrection should be always exhibited by them in connection with the ignominy of [Christ's] death.

JOHN CALVIN

JESUS CHRIST –
RISEN AND LIVING
(Continued)

The resurrection [is] the main proof of our Lord's Divinity.

If the resurrection is denied, all the apostolic language abut the atonement becomes a tissue of mystical exaggerations.

HENRY LIDDON

Easter Day . . . the birthday of the Church, as Pentecost was her baptism day.

ALFRED EDERSHEIM

'Christ is risen!' The resurrection of the body has already occurred! At least one resurrection body, that of Christ, already exists now.

OSCAR CULLMANN

JESUS CHRIST –
HIS ASCENSION

Jesus went away as regards His nature which is subject to local limitations, and remained in the world in respect of that nature which is ubiquitous. *Matt.* 28:20, ' Lo, I am with you alway . . . unto the end of the world.'

AUGUSTINE

The body which our Saviour has in heaven is the same as that which He had on earth.

Scripture everywhere teaches us that, as the Lord on earth took our humanity, so He has exalted it to heaven, withdrawing it from mortal condition, but not changing its nature.

JOHN CALVIN

The ends of His triumphant ascension [were]: 1. The overturning and destruction of all His enemies; 2. The preservation and continuation and rule of His church.

Heaven itself was not what it is, before the entrance of Christ into the sanctuary for the administration of His office.

JOHN OWEN

The ascension of Christ is not metaphorical and figurative.

The season of Christ's entrance into heaven . . . was the greatest instance of created glory that ever was or ever shall be.

When we look upon Him at the right hand of God, we see ourselves in heaven.

JOHN PEARSON

JESUS CHRIST –
MEDIATOR AND
INTERCESSOR

Thirty years ago [c.1520] this so remarkable an article of our faith, that Christ is our Advocate, was nearly buried.

For whom Christ died, for them also He rose again to make intercession for them ... these two acts of His priesthood are not to be separated.

The intercession of Christ is a continual application of His death for our salvation.

He continues still our advocate and spokesman at this day to procure us favour in God's sight.

Christ, by His death, purchased for Himself the honour of being the eternal advocate and peacemaker to present our prayer and our persons to the Father; to obtain supplies of grace for us, and enable us to hope we shall obtain what we ask.

JOHN CALVIN

Christ's prayer, *John* 17:17, is the blessed spring of our holiness; there is not anything in this grace wrought in us but what is so in answer to a compliance with the intercession of Christ.

JOHN OWEN

Christ presents His people's prayers to God . . . His precious merit, applied by His powerful intercession, purifies and perfects them. This skilful advocate puts them into form and language suited to the methods of the court of heaven and procures them a speedy hearing.

THOMAS BOSTON

He not only procures salvation, but also applies it. This special love wins its object, and rescues it.

GEORGE SMEATON

What Christ did for us sinners Godwards, was the fundamental part of His mediatorial work.

JAMES BUCHANAN

JESUS CHRIST – HIS PEOPLE'S PATTERN

Our Lord Jesus Christ . . . the Head, the Mirror and Pattern of all God's children.

In all our adversities we are shaped like to the image of our Lord Jesus Christ.

JOHN CALVIN

The life of God in us consists in conformity to Christ: nor is the Holy Spirit, as the principal and efficient cause of it, given to us for any other end but to unite us to Him, and make us like Him.

ANON.

JESUS CHRIST – ALL SUFFICIENT

In Jesus Christ we have all perfection. Thus we will be content with him alone.

Whatsoever our Lord Jesus Christ has, is all ours.

Since we see that the whole of our salvation and all the branches of it are comprehended in Christ, we must be cautious not to alienate from Him the least possible portion of it . . . If we seek redemption, it will be found in His passion;

JESUS CHRIST – ALL SUFFICIENT
(CONTINUED)

absolution, in His condemnation; remission of the curse, in His cross; satisfaction, in His sacrifice; purification, in His blood; reconciliation, in His descent into hell; mortification of the flesh, in His sepulchre; newness of life and immortality, in His resurrection; the inheritance of the celestial kingdom, in His entrance into heaven; protection, security, and enjoyment of all blessings, in His kingdom; a fearless expectation of the judgment in the judicial authority committed to Him.

JOHN CALVIN

This is the life and soul of all gospel comforts, that the whole inheritance of grace and glory is vested in Christ.

JOHN OWEN

JESUS CHRIST AND SCRIPTURE

Every prophet should be interpreted as speaking of Jesus Christ.

MARTIN LUTHER

The Old Testament . . . Christ's favourite book, Christ's only book! The book He always read and always quoted.

The whole life of the Saviour from His birth to His ascension may be narrated in the words of Moses and the prophets.

Only they who have received Christ have received Scripture as the Word of God.

JOHN CALVIN

Our Lord thus sets the seal of His authority upon the Genesis narrative, and does not recognize nor allow for any discrepancy between the concepts which were valid for Old Testament times and those valid for the fullness of the time when He spoke to His disciples, and still speaks to us.

JOHN MURRAY

At every point in our Lord's ministry the Old Testament was there in His heart, if not in His hands; in His thoughts if not in His words, determining the course that ministry should take, and providing the only possible language for its interpretation.

R. V. G. TASKER

The prophets, when they mention anything hard to be believed, are wont immediately afterwards to mention Christ; for in Him are ratified all the promises which would otherwise have been doubtful and uncertain (*2 Cor.*1:20).

Every doctrine of the law, every command, every promise, always points to Christ.

JOHN CALVIN

JESUS CHRIST IN HISTORY

The life and character of Jesus Christ is the holy of holies in the history of the world.

As the pyramids rise high above the sandy plains of Egypt, so Christ towers above all human teachers and founders of sects and religions.

PHILIP SCHAFF

Crucifixion: a Roman punishment, but, when the emperors themselves received Christianity, and the towering eagles resigned the flags unto the cross, this punishment was forbidden out of a due respect and pious honour to the death of Christ.

JOHN PEARSON

It was no part of the fathers at Chalcedon to invent a new doctrine, and the doctrine which they formulated had no single new element in it . . . It is only a very perfect synthesis of the biblical data.

B. B. WARFIELD

The man of Nazareth has, by universal consent, been the mightiest factor in our world's history; alike politically, socially, intellectually and morally.

ALFRED EDERSHEIM

The great passion of the human heart, until entirely conquered by the truth, is to reduce Jesus Christ to be only a name.

ALEXANDRE VINET

JESUS CHRIST – HIS RETURN

The mere effluxion of time has demonstrated [the second advent] to be a prodigious error.

THOMAS HUXLEY

Satan aims directly at the throat of the Church when he destroys faith in the coming of Christ.

It is the expectation of the final redemption alone that keeps us from growing weary. Let all who would persevere in a life of holiness give their whole minds to the hope of Christ's coming.

When we direct our eyes to this event the world is crucified to us, and we to the world.

Our life is hidden until our Lord Jesus Christ returns.

We must always be in readiness, and have, as it were, one foot lifted up to come to this blessed meeting of the Son of God.

Many things are referred to the latter day, at which time we shall see things fully and perfectly.

JOHN CALVIN

JESUS CHRIST – HIS RETURN
(CONTINUED)

Strictly speaking Christ will come, not for the destruction of the wicked, but for the purposes of salvation. This is the reason that the Creed mentions only the life of blessedness.

Just in proportion as men grow rampant in sin, may it be anticipated that the divine judgments are about to descend on them.

It is an extreme curse, when God gives us loose reins, and suffers us, with unbridled liberty, to rush as it were, headlong into evils, as though He had delivered us up to Satan to be his slaves.

Our faith cannot stand otherwise than by looking to the coming of Christ.

JOHN CALVIN

We Christians look to the future even more than to the present; it is part of our new nature to do so.

Next to the fact that Christ rose from the dead, the topic most frequently insisted upon in the apostolic writings is that He will come again from heaven.

HENRY LIDDON

Every passing minute brings us closer to the end point, and from the viewpoint of redemptive history, every passing moment is important in the Church.

The Risen One, when questioned by His disciples, rejects all questions regarding the 'when' of the kingdom of God.

OSCAR CULLMANN

Between [Christ's] ascension and His coming no event intervenes equal in importance to these. Therefore these two are joined together. Naturally then, the apostles . . . set before them the day of Christ as very near. And it accords with the majesty of Christ that during the whole period between His ascension and His advent He should, without intermission, be expected.

J. A. BENGEL

It is not for us to set an hour glass to the Creator of time.

SAMUEL RUTHERFORD

This world shall pass away by transmutation not by absolute destruction.

AUGUSTINE

JUDGMENT

John calls men to the lowly One, that they may not experience what He will be as the exalted Judge.

What will be His power when He comes to reign, who had this power when He came to die?

A – Z OF CHRISTIAN TRUTH AND EXPERIENCE

He was silent that He might be judged; he will not be silent when He begins to judge.

No one will judge more justly than He who was unjustly judged.

God loved Jacob of His unmerited grace, and hated Esau of his deserved judgment.

AUGUSTINE

We must set God before us on His judgment throne, and summon ourselves before Him, every morning and evening, knowing that we must give an account of our whole lives.

At the coming of our Lord Jesus Christ all books and registers shall be laid open, and nothing shall be hid any more . . . Therefore let us tarry patiently for that day.

The last judgment shall be nothing else than an approbation or ratification of the doctrine of the Gospel.

The Gospel cannot be certainly preached without summoning the whole world, as guilty, before the judgment seat of God.

God's judging of the world is not at our appointment.

It is not our business to question the judgments of God, before whose tribunal we must all hereafter stand.

Our Lord is fain to reserve the most part of things till His last judgment.

If the curse of God light on our heads, all the friendships in the world shall stand us in no stead.

Let us always endeavour to be established in the hope of the Last Judgment.

When God sends us word of His displeasure see we not how death is present at our backs?

The most part of such as shall be condemned at the last day, shall in this world escape the hands of the earthly judge.

JOHN CALVIN

There is nothing more certain in the Word of God, no doctrine more clear and fundamental, than that of eternal judgment.

JOHN PEARSON

I am content to wait till the Judgment Day for the clearing of my character; and after I am dead I desire no other epitaph than this: Here lies George Whitefield; what sort of man he was the great day will discover.

GEORGE WHITEFIELD

He heard the wheels of an avenging God
Groan heavily along the distant road.

WILLIAM COWPER

JUDGMENT
(Continued)

The guilt of rejecting Christ cannot be fully appreciated until that day when He shall sit on His throne.

In judgment Christ will draw a sharp, trenchant line of eternal separation through the dense throng of all the assemblies, races and generations of men.

Justice is wholly unsatisfied within the limits of this earthly existence.

HENRY LIDDON

So long as the idea of responsibility is still free from the idea of the Last Judgment, it is still harmless, it is merely a dream of responsibility.

EMIL BRUNNER

JUSTICE

[God] loved Jacob of His undeserved grace and hated Esau of His deserved judgment.

Without justice what are kingdoms but great banditries?

AUGUSTINE

He who has defaced justice is guilty of treason against God.

Civic justice [is] a little mirror of God's justice; worldly justice a little spark of God's justice.

There is no other means to be in right freedom than to be held in awe under God and His justice.

[*On the Roman Emperor Nerva's government*] It is bad to live under a prince who permits nothing, but much worse to live under one who permits everything.

Without the sword laws are dead.

As long as men presume to murmur against God, and to blaspheme His justice; they must have as many deadly enemies as there are angels in heaven.

Justice consists in yielding every man his right; judgment consents not to any evils, nor suffers the poor to be misused.

There is, as it were, an inseparable knot between God's justice and our salvation.

We must never seek the execution of God's justice in this world, for that were an evil principle.

JOHN CALVIN

Justice – the self-asserting activity according to which He maintains the inalienable rights of the Godhead.

GEORGE SMEATON

Every sin will be adequately punished; blessed be God, not every sinner.

JOHN DUNCAN

A man who has no adequate sense of the evil of sin, cannot believe in the justice of God.

CHARLES HODGE

A – Z OF CHRISTIAN TRUTH AND EXPERIENCE

Many literalize and emphasize [God's] love, but convert [His] wrath into metaphor and hyperbole.

WILLIAM G. T. SHEDD

Man will not rest in God's judgment concerning him but he seeks for rest in his own estimate of himself.

The ethical idea is: I am sick, how can I become well? The juridical idea is: How can God's violated right be restored?

Sin and guilt belong together . . . Confounding sin and guilt must lead to confounding justification and sanctification.

ABRAHAM KUYPER

Against my will I was compelled to acknowledge that collective man was incapable, not merely of ideal perfection, but of mere justice.

D. R. DAVIES

JUSTIFICATION [1]

O sweet exchange! O unfathomable work of God! O blessings beyond all expectation! The sinfulness of man is hidden in the Righteous One, while the righteousness of the One justifies the many that are sinners.

THE EPISTLE TO DIOGNETUS (late second century)

Justification by faith . . . the article of a standing or a falling church.

MARTIN LUTHER

[1] See also ATONEMENT and JESUS CHRIST — OBEDIENCE AND DEATH

Satan had laboured at nothing more assiduously than to extinguish, or to smother the gratuitous justification of faith, which is here asserted. (*Gen.* 15:6) . . . Abraham obtained righteousness . . . by imputation.

The righteousness of faith is so exceedingly different from that of works, that if the one be established, the other must necessarily be subverted.

The whole dispute is as to the cause of Justification . . . However small the portion attributed to our work, to that extent faith will waver and our whole salvation be endangered.

A man cannot be justified by faith unless he has first recognized and acknowledged in complete sincerity that he is lost.

An acceptance by which God receives us into His favour, and esteems us as righteous persons . . . it consists in the remission of sins, and the imputation of the righteousness of Christ.

JOHN CALVIN

Justification is an act of God's free grace, wherein he pardoneth all our sins, and accepteth us as righteous in His sight, only for the righteousness of Christ imputed to us, and received by faith alone.

WESTMINSTER SHORTER CATECHISM, *Answer 33*

JUSTIFICATION
(CONTINUED)

Cain wrote his indignation against justification . . . by faith, in the blood of his brother.

THOMAS BOSTON

I would have every preacher insist on these two doctrines – a present justification by grace through faith alone, and a future justification according to works.

THOMAS CHALMERS

Condemnation is a sentence of death pronounced upon sin; justification is a sentence of life pronounced upon righteousness.

CHARLES HODGE

This article of Justification is that which forms the church, nourishes it, builds it up, preserves and defends it. It is the heel which crushes the serpent's head.

We are justified by faith . . . but faith is not itself the righteousness on account of which we are justified.

As the ground of justification the Roman Catholic Church substituted the inherent righteousness of the regenerate for the imputed righteousness of the Redeemer.

Roman Catholic Justification virtually substitutes the work of the Spirit in us for the work of Christ for us.

JAMES BUCHANAN

Justification by faith is the Thermopylae of Christianity.

CHARLES H. SPURGEON

Justification works *for* man; sanctification *in* man. Justification removes the guilt; sanctification the stain. Justification imputes to us an extraneous righteousness; sanctification works righteousness inherent as our own. Justification is at once completed; sanctification increases gradually, hence remains imperfect.

Man's case, in relation to God, must be considered juridically. Be not afraid of that word, brother. Rather insist that it be pronounced with as strong an emphasis as possible.

ABRAHAM KUYPER

[Eastern] Orthodox theology makes justification a process linked with sanctification in which man is gradually made righteous by infused grace, or transformed into a quasi-divine condition.

W. NIESEL

The New Testament never says that a man is saved on account of his faith, but always that he is saved through faith. Faith is the means which the Holy Spirit uses to apply to the soul the benefits of Christ's death.

J. GRESHAM MACHEN

If justification is confounded with regeneration or sanctification then the door is opened for the perversion of the gospel at its centre.

In the Scripture justification is never said to be *dia pistin* (Greek, *on account of faith*).

JOHN MURRAY

KNOWLEDGE

He lives ill who does not believe well concerning God.

AUGUSTINE

True substantial wisdom principally consists of two parts, the knowledge of God and the knowledge of ourselves.

The knowledge of God is efficacious . . . To know Him is immediately to love Him.

JOHN CALVIN

THE LAW

[Sinners] inveterately hate the law itself, and execrate God the law giver.

AUGUSTINE

The tables [of the law] were written not on one side only, but on both, even to the full . . . that no man living should add anything to them.

The true performance of the Law begins at the loving of God.

True wisdom manifests itself in the observance of the law.

Contempt of the law of God is the source of everything bad.

We must resort to our Lord Jesus Christ whose office is to write the things in our hearts which God had written in stones.

It belongs only to God to judge whether we be good or evil . . . God will judge our works by the trial of His law . . . He will not devise a new judgment; but He has given us His law. God is both the lawgiver, and also the judge.

The peculiar office of the Law is to summon conscience to the judgment-seat of God.

When He brings us to the law, and condemns us, it is not for His own profit, but for our salvation and wealth.

Has God set anything down in the two tables [of the Law] which He has not always written by the Holy Spirit in the hearts of His children?

JOHN CALVIN

God will multiply pardon; but modify and take down His law, never!

JOHN DUNCAN

We have never, in any one moment of our lives, been or done what the law requires us to be or do.

The knowledge of sin is derived from the law . . . because it is an

THE LAW

expression of the perfect holiness of God.

CHARLES HODGE

The term curse expresses the penal sanction of the law [of God].

GEORGE SMEATON

LEADERS

Such men are raised to station and command,
When Providence means mercy to a land.
He speaks, and they appear; to Him they owe
Skill to direct and strength to strike the blow.

WILLIAM COWPER

LEARNING

Vast erudition is quite compatible with moral obliquity.

AUGUSTINE

However good an opinion the princes of this world have of their own shrewdness, we may be sure they are arrant fools till they become humble scholars at the feet of Christ.

No learning is commendable which is not dipped in the love of God.

JOHN CALVIN

LITERATURE

Only a spiritually minded-church

provides the soil in which a literature of the Spirit can grow.

B. B. WARFIELD

There is great intellectual ability in the pulpit of our day, great scholarship, great eloquence, and great earnestness, but spiritual preaching, preaching to the spirit – 'wet-eyed' preaching – is a lost art. At the same time, if that living art is for the present overlaid and lost, the literature of a deeper spiritual day abides with us, and our spiritually-minded people are not confined to us, they are not dependent on us.

ALEXANDER WHYTE

LITURGY

For the first two or three centuries there were no systems of composed forms of prayer used in any church whatever.

Prayer is God's institution . . . The Spirit of God helps us to pray, not to make prayers.

JOHN OWEN

When the spirit of prayer began to be lost, then forms of prayer were invented, and, I believe, the same observation will hold good as to preaching.

GEORGE WHITEFIELD

The theory of Presbyterianism is opposed to the use of liturgies . . . The compulsory use of liturgies is, and has ever been felt to be, inconsistent with the liberty wherewith Christ has made us free.

There are no indications of the use of liturgies in the New Testament. There is no evidence of the use of written forms during the first three centuries.

CHARLES HODGE

THE LORD'S DAY [1]

On the day called Sunday there is a meeting in one place . . . and the memoirs of the apostles or the writings of the prophets are read.

JUSTIN MARTYR

The Lord's Day must serve us for a tower to mount up into to view God's works afar off . . . the minding thereof will fashion and polish us . . . to yield thanks on Monday and all the week after. It is necessary to have one special day dedicated wholly thereunto.

JOHN CALVIN

It was called 'the Lord's Day' because it was appointed and set apart by Him, from common to a sacred use, and to be observed according to His appointment, in commemoration of the work of redemption, which is a greater and more glorious work than the work of creation.

A. S. PATERSON

Though under Christian liberty the ceremonial Sabbath is done away in

[1] See also THE SABBATH

Christ, the rest day is continued in the Lord's Day observance of the completion of the New Creation in the Resurrection Life.

S. R. MACPHAIL

Sir Frances Drake in three years' sailing about the world lost only one Sunday's observance.

THOMAS FULLER

Sunday is the sun of days when light and warmth are diffused over the week.

CHRISTOPH LUTHARDT

THE LORD'S SUPPER

There are two memorial ordinances in the New Testament, and there are only two, the Lord's supper and the Lord's day. The one celebrates the Lord's death, the other his resurrection. It is most significant that this should be the case. These are the pivotal events of redemption. The Lord's day is ever recurrent and the Lord's supper should be frequently administered. 'As often as ye eat this bread' (*1 Cor.*11:26).

JOHN MURRAY

LOVE

Your accord and harmonious love is a hymn to Jesus Christ.

IGNATIUS

I mean by love that affection of the mind which aims at the enjoyment of God for His own sake and the

LOVE
(Continued)

enjoyment of oneself and one's neighbour in subordination to God.

[*On John 13:34,35*] 'As He . . . has loved us.' This is the love that renews us, making us new men, heirs of the New Testament, singers of the new song . . . That love is our death to the world, and our life with God.

Two cities have been formed by two loves; the earthly by the love of self, even to the contempt of God; the heavenly by the love of God, even to the contempt of self.

Augustine

Augustine speaks of 'My tongue and my pen, yoked together in me, with love as the charioteer'.

Love fears and is concerned for the beloved. What is not loved is easily neglected.

Martin Luther

Them that are good I love, because they are in Christ; and the evil, to bring them to Christ.

Christ is the cause why I love thee, why I am ready to do the uttermost of my power for thee, and why I pray for thee.

William Tyndale

[*On 1 Corinthians 8:1*] Whatever is devoid of love is of no account in the sight of God.

Without love . . . all our services shall be refused as unprofitable.

Love forms the chief part of Christian perfection.

Truly we must not love God as our fellow or mate; but we must stand in awe of Him.

[*On Psalm 18:1*] Love to God is here laid down as constituting the principal part of true godliness . . . for we are bound fast to Him by the chain of a free and spontaneous love.

Mutual love among ministers is demanded above all things, that they may be employed with one accord in building up the Church of God. If ministers do not maintain brotherly intercourse with each other . . . there will be no building up of the Church.

In order to preserve love we must bear with many things.

Let him who would engage in the duties of love prepare himself for a life of labour.

The conquerors of all temptations are those who love God.

John Calvin

I am so in love with His love that if His love were not in heaven I should be unwilling to go thither.

Samuel Rutherford

The love of Christ in the soul takes the very nails that fastened Him to the cross, and crucifies the soul to the world and to sin.

It is the powerful love of Christ which kills the love of sin, and kindles the love of holiness in the soul.

No greater gift can be given to Christ than His people's love . . . the reflex of Christ's love to them.

Where His love is no other incentive will be needful.

Self-love is the perfect opposite to the love of God.

ROBERT LEIGHTON

Nothing renders us so like to God as our love to Jesus Christ.

Love, proceeding from sight, is the life of the Church above, as love proceeding from faith is the life of the Church below.

In this world believers are united to God by faith; in heaven by love.

[God] implanted love in our nature to express this eternal mutual love of the holy persons of the Trinity.

To love God is the only way and means to be like Him.

Love, proceeding from faith, gradually changes the soul, into the likeness of God; and the more it is in exercise the more is that change effected.

JOHN OWEN

[*On Ephesians 3:18–19*] To be ravished with love, affected with love, always thinking of love, speaking of love, expressing this sense of love, that is a work behoving saints.

THOMAS MANTON

In the Person of Jesus Christ all the discordances are harmonized.

The God of Christians is a God who makes the soul feel that He is its only good; that its repose is wholly in Him; that its only joy is in loving Him, and who, at the same time makes it hate everything that seduces it and keeps it from loving Him with all its powers.

BLAISE PASCAL

[*On Ephesians 3:19*] This love of Christ has entered the apostle's heart; he was swallowed up in the meditation and admiration of it, and would have all hearts inflamed and affected with it, as his was.

JOHN FLAVEL

'Tis truth divine exhibited on
  earth,
Gives charity her being and her
  birth.

WILLIAM COWPER

If the life of the heart is to love, the heart is dead when we love self only; and dead when we hate.

ALEXANDRE VINET

LOVE
(CONTINUED)

The true reward of loving is to love yet more.

Selfishness has no leisure. We have little time when we have little love. Silence, meditation, a view of heaven, a serious and austere life, are all needed in order to love.

ALEXANDRE VINET

There is no duty more frequently and pointedly enjoined in the New Testament than love of the brethren.

CHARLES HODGE

Irenaeus (*On Heresies*) includes love among the notes of the church, just after he has spoken of schism. Augustine used this weapon against the Donatists. Their lack of *caritas* (love) proves they have not the Holy Spirit. Therefore, they cannot be the church.

S. L. GREENSLADE

THE LOVE OF GOD

All our salvation and the praise thereof, must be shut up within the simple love of God.

The source and origin of the church is the free love of God.

Our minds cannot find calm repose until we arrive at the unmerited love of God.

What is the reason why He pours innumerable blessings upon us, in constant succession, unless that, having once embraced us with paternal love, He cannot deny Himself.

God does love all people, but yet not in comparison of His Church . . . those whom He has chosen . . . for His children.

Albeit God loves all people, yet His saints are in His charge or protection, even those whom He has chosen.

God's love is printed in our hearts by His Holy Spirit.

JOHN CALVIN

It is not so much the threatenings of the law but the apprehension of the love of God which turns the sinner from his rebellion, and draws him back to submission and obedience.

CHARLES HODGE

MAN IN SIN

Why is it that we remember with difficulty and without difficulty forget? learn with difficulty and without difficulty remain ignorant? are diligent with difficulty and without difficulty are indolent?

AUGUSTINE

Worldlings cannot be merry but when they forget God.

Unbelieving and irreligious men have no ears.

JOHN CALVIN

The world is full of fugitives from themselves.

ALEXANDRE VINET

Man always believes more readily that which he prefers.

JOHN DUNCAN

Guilt, like fear, is a sense of home-lessness – of being cast out of one's own home and for one's own fault.

EMIL BRUNNER

MEDITATION

He alone has made solid proficiency in the Gospel who has been accus-tomed to continual meditation on the blessed resurrection.

JOHN CALVIN

Meditation is different from study-ing. By study, truth is explored; by meditation it is felt. By the one, things different are discriminated; by the other, what is known is loved and embraced. The design of secret meditation is not so much to accum-ulate knowledge, or to please our-selves, as to enlarge the desires of the soul and to elevate the affections.

DAVID STURROCK

I take a walk every day, by faith and meditation, to mount Calvary; there is nothing like it.

MATTHEW HENRY

I derive my whole consolation from meditating on the Godhead and character of Jesus Christ, in whom I place all my confidence.

RICHARD CECIL

MEEKNESS

Study meekness, for the glory and advantage of the truth. It needs not the service of passion.

ROBERT LEIGHTON

Meekness in our Lord was not a weak bearing of evils, but a strong forbearance in the presence of evil.

B. B. WARFIELD

MEMORIZING SCRIPTURE

[In our study of the Scriptures] we should commit them to memory . . . Memory counts for a great deal; if memory be defective no rules can supply the want.

AUGUSTINE

[*On Origen's debt to his Christian father*] He every day required him to learn passages by heart and repeat them aloud.

EUSEBIUS

Let us learn to exercise ourselves in His promises, early and late, and to renew the remembrance of them. This remembrance of God's stat-utes has an invigorating effect.

JOHN CALVIN

MEMORIZING SCRIPTURE
(CONTINUED)

Walked from Hyde Park corner repeating the 119th Psalm.

WILLIAM WILBERFORCE

Angelique Arnaud knew the Psalter by heart at the age of nine.

THE STORY OF PORT ROYAL

The early missionaries to the New Hebrides in the Western Pacific (now the independent Republic of Vanuatu) found that the new converts took to the memorization of Scripture with ease. Dr and Mrs Gunn were on lonely Fotuna Island from 1882. Her young woman's class began to memorize the Scriptures. She promised a new frock to any who memorized Jonah. Twelve frocks were claimed. On Tanna Dr J. Campbell Nicholson had his class memorize the Shorter Catechism in the local language. They repeated the 107 answers, some without a mistake. That was in 1912. Mrs Gunn's girls went on to memorize John's Gospel.

J. GRAHAM MILLER

Language was my great difficulty in early life. I had not natural command of words. I undertook to remedy the defect by committing to memory large portions of the New Testament, the Psalms, and much of the Prophets.

JAMES HENLEY THORNWELL

MEN-PLEASING

God strongly exhorts those whose duty it is to preach the Word not to seek grace and favour in the eyes of men.

Nothing has a more powerful tendency to withdraw teachers from a faithful and upright dispensation of the Word than to pay respect to men.

JOHN CALVIN

THE MIND – FALLEN

[On John chapter 9] The blind man is the human race . . . every man is born mentally blind.

AUGUSTINE

There is no other division or heresy in the world save man's wisdom and when man's foolish wisdom interprets the Scriptures.

WILLIAM TYNDALE

So thoroughly infected is the mind of man with a depraved curiosity, that the greater part of men are always gaping after new revelations.

The human mind has a natural inclination towards vanity and errors.

Man's mind is like a store of idolatry and superstition.

There is nothing more deadly than to lean to our own wisdom. Satan has so many devices by which he deludes and blinds men's minds,

A – Z OF CHRISTIAN TRUTH AND EXPERIENCE

that there is not a man who knows the hundredth part of his own sins.

We know nothing vainer than the minds of men.

JOHN CALVIN

The absence of the Spirit has . . . left the mind in moral and spiritual impotence. If regard be had to the understanding, the unconverted cannot know the things of the Spirit of God (*1 Cor.* 2:14); to the will, he cannot be subject to the law of God (*Rom.* 8:7); to worship, he cannot please God (*Rom.* 8:8); to fruit, he cannot bear fruit (*John* 15:4); to faith, he cannot receive the Spirit of truth (*John* 14:17).

JOHN HOWE

We are heart-atheists by nature.

SAMUEL RUTHERFORD

Through our wretched apostasy from God, our mind is become the seat and habitation of all vanity, disorder and confusion.

It is an evidence of corruption of nature that it disenables the minds of men to discern their own corruption.

JOHN OWEN

The whole course of a man's life out of Christ, is nothing but a continual trading in vanity.

ROBERT LEIGHTON

In proportion, as men are corrupt they are blind.

CHARLES HODGE

Sin has its seat in the very centre of the intellectual consciousness of man.

AUGUSTE LECERF

Our reason, apart from its restoration by the Word of grace, is always sinfully self-sufficient, a reason infected with rationalism and unbelief.

It is not the animal instincts but the mind of man which is the origin of all evil; this same mind, this same heart, is the fiery abyss whence issues all that is demonic and destructive.

EMIL BRUNNER

MIRACLES

A miracle is the intervention of God's grace in act; prophecy is the intervention of God's grace in testimony.

ADOLPH SAPHIR

MODESTY

A mature knowledge of things makes a man modest.

Whence comes modesty but from the Holy Ghost? Till our Lord enlightens us by His Word, we are utterly devoid of all discretion, and there is neither modesty nor honesty in us.

Those who have confessed themselves before God to be such as

MODESTY
(Continued)

they are, will also have the modesty of not justifying themselves before men.

Reverence always begets modesty.

JOHN CALVIN

Thou art never bidden to believe in thyself.

ROBERT LEIGHTON

MURDER

God curses whole countries for the suffering of murders . . . God sets great store by men's lives. He takes [murder] as an assault on Himself in His own Person, and in His own majesty.

JOHN CALVIN

MUSIC

Flute and taber and such other like things are not to be condemned simply of their own nature, but only in respect of men's abusing of them.

JOHN CALVIN

When not plain and simple, it may delight the ear, and imagination, but it obstructs the true melody of the heart.

J. A. BENGEL

Music, written primarily for the joy of making music, remains secular, no matter what its ostensible purpose.

G. R. CRAGG

MYSTERY

There is light enough for those who are disposed to see, and darkness enough for those who are disinclined. There is illumination sufficient to inform the elect, and obscurity sufficient to humble them. There is obscurity sufficient to prevent the reprobate from seeing, and illumination sufficient to condemn them and render them inexcusable.

BLAISE PASCAL

The Three Mystical Unions, which are the chief mysteries in religion: 1. The union of the Trinity of Persons in one Godhead. 2. The union of the divine and human natures in one Person, Jesus Christ, God and man. 3. The union of Christ with the believer.

WALTER MARSHALL

None of us shall be able to answer the question why one was chosen to be a vessel of honour and another was left as a vessel of wrath.

ABRAHAM KUYPER

Mystery is the mark which the infinite Being has placed upon His work, and it judges reason. Mystery is the atmosphere necessary to the religious life.

AUGUSTE LECERF

OBEDIENCE

Obedience rests on faith, as faith does on the Word.

JOHN CALVIN

Faith in the Person of Christ is the spring of all evangelical obedience.

JOHN OWEN

OCCUPATIONS

God will only approve of occupations which are profitable and serviceable to the whole community.

Every individual has his own kind of living assigned to him by the Lord as a sort of sentry post so that he may not heedlessly wander about throughout life . . . no task will be so sordid and base, provided you obey your calling in it, that it will not shine and be reckoned very precious in God's sight.

Let God's servants learn to measure carefully their powers, lest they should wear out by ambitiously embracing too many occupations. For this propensity to engage in too many things is a very common malady . . . God has so arranged our condition that individuals are only endued with a certain measure of gifts.

God has put us into the world to keep us occupied in His service.

JOHN CALVIN

[As] for a mere contemplative life, which terminates in itself and sends out no rays either of light or of heat into human society, theology knows it not.

FRANCIS BACON

What have we our time and strength for, but to lay both out for God? What is a candle made but to burn? He that works much lives much.

RICHARD BAXTER

Disparagement of the body (which is closely associated with the disparagement of manual labour) is essentially a pagan attitude.

M. C. V. JEFFREYS

The fundamental method of doing good works is the fulfilling of one's calling.

W. STANFORD REID

God has a plan for every life surrendered to Him.

ROWLAND BINGHAM

We must guard against evidently useless enterprises.

ALEXANDRE VINET

PATIENCE

It is a very hard piece of work to build the Church of God, and cannot be brought to pass in one day . . . for one man's life is not sufficient for it.

JOHN CALVIN

PATIENCE
(CONTINUED)

Greatly shall they have profited in God's school, who can hold themselves in quiet, and not attempt more than God has commanded.

Patience is the fruit and proof of faith.

Let us not find it strange that the kingdom is so small now, and not taken into account, openly opposed and seemingly will never be advanced . . . This is for the best . . . Let us wait in patience until His kingdom be established in perfection.

JOHN CALVIN

PENTECOST

With the powerful co-operation of heaven the whole world was suddenly lit by the sunshine of the saving Word . . . In every town and village, like a well-filled threshing floor, churches shot up bursting with eager members.

EUSEBIUS

[Pentecost was] a kind of renewing of the whole world, to exalt the kingdom of our Lord Jesus Christ, for there He uttered His power, yea more than He did in His resurrection. For what had we been the better for Christ's rising again in His own Person, if He had not poured out the grace of His Holy Spirit upon His church, to show that He was set at the right hand of God His Father, to fill all things and to dwell in us, and that He has such sovereign dominion over all things?

JOHN CALVIN

This 'pouring out' (*Acts* 2) has respect unto the gifts and graces of the Spirit, and not to His Person; for where He is given, He is given absolutely, and as to Himself, not more or less; but His gifts and graces may be more plentifully and abundantly given at one time than another, to some persons than to others.

JOHN OWEN

The effect on the disciples was most marked . . . self-consciousness, self-questioning, self-doubting, self-glorying seem to have fled.

J. ELDER CUMMING

The Day of Pentecost sealed the testimony of Easter.

BROOKE FOSS WESCOTT

PERFECTIONISM

We never do any good in which there is not some blemish.

JOHN CALVIN

PERSECUTION

Persecutions are, in a manner, seals of adoption to the children of God.

JOHN CALVIN

PHILOSOPHY

Philosophy, however enlightened, however profound, gives no command over the passions, no influential motives, no vivifying principles.

JOHN HENRY NEWMAN

PRAISE

Confession of sin all know, but to confession of praise few attend.

AUGUSTINE

Only a new man can sing a new song. A person cannot praise God unless he understand that there is nothing in himself worthy of praise, but that all is of God and from God.

To remember means always to praise.

MARTIN LUTHER

We only praise God aright when we are filled and overwhelmed with an ecstatic admiration of the immensity of His power.

Praise constitutes the chief exercise of godliness in which God would have us to be engaged during the whole of our life.

The whole world is a theatre for the display of the divine goodness, wisdom, justice and power, but the church is the orchestra, as it were, the most conspicuous part of it.

The most holy service we can render to God is to be employed in praising His name.

JOHN CALVIN

What are our lame praises in comparison of His love? Nothing! but love will stammer rather than be dumb.

It is spiritual knowledge of God that sets the soul in tune for His praises.

ROBERT LEIGHTON

A line of praise is worth a page of prayer.

JOHN LIVINGSTONE

Praise is the element of heaven . . . Self forgotten, it is the Lamb that is remembered.

ANDREW BONAR

PRAYER

Before praying, give thanks, and before teaching, pray.

The intellect makes the prayer, but the feeling makes the cry.

MARTIN LUTHER

[Prayer is] an earnest and familiar talking with God.

JOHN KNOX

[Christ] speaks on my behalf, and I approach God in His name, as if I were the Lord Jesus Christ Himself . . . united to Him.

JOHN CALVIN

PRAYER
(CONTINUED)

The Holy Ghost seals our adoption, to the end we may cry Abba, Father, whereby we are sure He will hear us.

Prayer is the only witness to show whether we have faith or not.

It is the Holy Spirit alone who works us into that frame wherein we pray continually . . . by giving an ability for prayer, or communicating a gift unto the minds of men.

Do we anything in all our prayers, than charge God with His promises? And so now we go into the sanctuary of heaven to present ourselves before the face of God.

The prayers that we offer are, as it were, keys by which to come to the treasures that God reserves for us.

There is nothing more efficacious in our prayers than to set His own Word before God and then to found our supplication upon His promises, as if He dictated to us out of His own mouth what we were to ask.

Unless the promises of God shine on us, and invite us to prayer, no sincere prayer can ever be drawn from us.

We cannot pray without the Word . . . leading the way. Thus everyone who has no faith in the promises prays dissemblingly.

The invocation of God's name is His peculiar work; for men do not pray through the suggestion of the flesh, but when God draws them.

We are permitted to pour into God's bosom the difficulties which torment us, in order that He may loosen the knots we cannot untie.

We cannot possibly exercise true confidence in prayer, except by resting firmly on God's Word.

In prayer two things are necessary, faith and humility; by faith we rise up to God, and by humility we lie prostrate on the ground.

The test of faith lies in prayer.

Genuine and earnest prayer proceeds first from a sense of our need and next from faith in the promises of God.

The sole end and legitimate use of prayer [is] that we may reap the fruits of God's promises.

Prayers flow from doctrine.

The discipline of the cross is necessary so that earnest prayer may become vigorous in us.

The finest rhetoric and the best grace which we can have before Him consists in pure simplicity.

The answer of our prayers is secured by the fact that in rejecting them He would, in a sense, deny His own nature.

We can pray with confidence if we know that the Lord Jesus Christ is our Mediator.

Grant, Almighty God, that as we are wholly nothing, and less than nothing, we may know our nothingness, and having cast away all confidence in the world, as well as in ourselves, we may learn to flee to Thee as suppliants.

When overtaken by adversity we are ever to conclude that it is a rod of correction sent by God to stir us up to pray.

Our own scanty desires hinder God from pouring out His gifts upon us in greater abundance.

As oft as we pray let us begin at the promises.

It is good to have certain hours appointed for prayer, not because we are tied to hours, but lest we be unmindful of prayer.

When we come to make our prayers to God we must not bring thither with us our melancholy passions and fretting and fuming . . . We must pray to God with a peaceable heart.

Except God shines on us by His Word, we cannot come to Him; faith is ever the mother of prayer.

The modesty of faith consists in permitting God to appoint differently from our desires.

God can easily turn our prayers into bread.

Our own impatience shuts the gate against our prayers.

God furthers our soul's health in refusing to grant us the things that He knows to be unmeet for us.

[Christ] has set it down as a rule in praying to God that we must call Him our Father (*Matt.* 6:9).

Let us learn, when we feel sluggish and cold in prayer, to collect all the aids that can arouse our feelings, and correct the torpor of which we are conscious.

Kneeling in time of prayer is a sign of humility.

[God] regards our prayers as the chief and supreme sacrifice, by which we do homage to His Majesty.

JOHN CALVIN

To pray is *ars artium*, an art above all arts.

Christ looks not to the work of praying but to the heart of the prayer.

HUGH LATIMER

Desire and depend upon the assistance and inspiration of the Holy Spirit of God.

Offer not to speak to Him without the heart . . . seasoned . . . with the sense of His greatness and holiness.

ROBERT LEIGHTON

PRAYER
(CONTINUED)

If you would have easy and sweet access to God in prayer: seek a holy heart, seek a broken heart, seek a humble heart

ROBERT LEIGHTON

Our prayers are an extract and copy of the work of the Holy Spirit in us, given us by Himself.

JOHN OWEN

Prayers not felt by us are seldom heard by God.

PHILIP HENRY

The bride ought to be frequent in sending posts and messages to her blessed bridegroom . . . and no letter sent to him, so short or ill-written, but he will read it.

JAMES DURHAM

Those who had most of the spirit of prayer were all to be found in gaol; and those who had most of the form of prayer were all to be found at the alehouse.

CHARLES STANFORD,
on Joseph Alleine and the Great
Ejection of 1662

There is in some persons a most unsuitable and insufferable boldness in their addresses to the great Jehovah, in an ostentation of eminent nearness and familiarity.

JONATHAN EDWARDS

There are many prayers not to be answered till we come to the other world (*Rom.* 7:24).

The Lord's Prayer is given us as a directory for prayer, a pattern and an example – respecting the matter of our petitions – rather than a form.

The voice is of good use in secret prayer to stir up the affections, and to stay the mind from wandering.

THOMAS BOSTON

The standard by which to estimate our true condition is the degree in which we are conversant with prayer.

The first essential in the Christian life is prayer, and the second is love to Holy Scripture, and living in it.

CRISTOPH LUTHARDT

The child of God has great privileges, but the greatest of all is to learn how to supplicate.

He that prays is nearer to Jesus Christ than the apostles were.

ALEXANDRE VINET

Speaking of his mother after her death:
I never forget the firmness and regularity with which she kept to herself the morning hour for being alone after breakfast, and the hour before evening worship: this struck me as a boy.

ANDREW BONAR

Mere mental prayer is necessarily imperfect; earnest, fervent prayer constrains us to express it in words.

ABRAHAM KUYPER

A – Z OF CHRISTIAN TRUTH AND EXPERIENCE

Three directions for prayer: Pray till you pray; pray till you are conscious of being heard; pray till you receive an answer.

ALEXANDER MOODY STUART

We hold that the purposes of God are not changed, but what if prayer be a part of His purpose, and what if He ordains that His people should pray when He intends to give them blessings? Prayer is one of the necessary wheels of the machinery of providence. God in very truth hearkens to the voices of men.

CHARLES H. SPURGEON

Twelve Hebrew words have been rendered by the English word 'pray' in the Old Testament.

R. B. GIRDLESTONE

Prayer is the cry of a non-entity, lost in the immensity of the universe on this speck of dust which we call the earth, sent up to the sovereign Being, trusting in His promise, believing that nothing can be too great for His power, and nothing too small for His pity.

AUGUSTE LECERF

Always respond to any impulse to pray.

D. MARTYN LLOYD-JONES

PRAYER AND THE CHRISTIAN MINISTRY

The Christian teacher should pray before preaching – He will succeed more by piety in prayer than by gifts of oratory.

AUGUSTINE

These two things are united, teaching and praying; God would have him whom He has set as a teacher in His Church, to be assiduous in prayer.

That the greater part of teachers [that is, ministers] either languish through indolence, or utterly give way through despair, arises from nothing else than that they are sluggish in the duty of prayer.

JOHN CALVIN

This one ordinance shuts us all up to a very peculiar necessity of becoming and continuing to be men of prayer.

ALEXANDER MOODY STUART

I think that we are to be content to labour little comparatively, if we cannot water all that with abundant prayer.

ANDREW BONAR

PREACHERS AND PREACHING

God commands us to will that all to whom we preach this peace may be saved, and Himself works this in us by diffusing that love in our hearts by the Holy Spirit who is given to us.

AUGUSTINE

PREACHERS AND PREACHING

(CONTINUED)

Keep not silent, O Lord, concerning the resurrection of the flesh; lest men believe it not, and we continue reasoners, not preachers.

AUGUSTINE

Christ acts by them in such a manner that he wishes their mouth to be reckoned as His mouth, and their lips as His lips.

No man can know how to speak one word to the glory of Jesus Christ except it is given him, and that the Holy Ghost govern his tongue.

The glory of God so shines in His Word, that we ought to be so affected by it, whenever He speaks by His servants, as though He were nigh us, face to face.

It is very difficult to preach in all simplicity that which is contained in the Word of God without encountering much conflict.

We must speak of God's law much more with our hearts than with our mouths.

To all the ministers of the Word . . . is given such efficacy of the Word, that they may not idly beat the air with their voices, but may reach the hearts, and touch them to the quick.

God has nothing else in view in addressing men but to call them to salvation.

JOHN CALVIN

Preaching must not be allowed to decay, for surely if preaching decay, ignorance and brutishness will enter again.

HUGH LATIMER

It is one thing to bring truth from the Bible and another thing to bring it from God Himself, through the Bible.

ANDREW BONAR

Without knowing something of the power of the Holy Spirit [the ministry] is a heart-breaking task.

D. MARTYN LLOYD-JONES

Much evangelical preaching suffers from the absence in the preacher himself of the note of contrition and humility.

The demonstration and power of the Holy Spirit is an accompanying operation of the Spirit, supplementary to the word of the gospel . . . It is an additional attestation, indispensable to the faith that rests on the power of God.

JOHN MURRAY

PREDESTINATION

Christ's church has never failed to hold the faith of this predestination which is now being defended with new solicitude against these modern heretics.

AUGUSTINE

I believe that this faith and belief in Christ is the . . . gift of God, that is to those whom God the Father, before the beginning of the world hath predestinated in Christ unto eternal life.

If you feel not this faith, then know that predestination is too high a matter for you to be disputers of it until you have been better scholars in the school-house of repentance and justification.

JOHN BRADFORD

So God predestinated, not because He foresaw men *would* be conformed to Christ, but that they *might* be so.

ROBERT LEIGHTON

I believe in predestination without cutting and trimming it, and I believe in responsibility without adulterating and weakening it.

CHARLES H. SPURGEON

Wycliffe defines the church militant as 'the body of the predestinate, while it is here journeying to its home'.

JAMES CANDLISH

In no doctrine is the 'Soli Deo gloria' more demanded of us than in our thought of predestination.

JOHN MURRAY

PRESUMPTION

I see many leaky vessels fair before the wind, who take their conversion on trust, and they go on securely and see not the underwater till a storm sink them.

SAMUEL RUTHERFORD

[Every Christian needs] that cautious spirit, that great sense of the vast importance of a sure foundation, and that dread of being deceived.

A trust in God in the way of negligence is what in Scripture is called tempting God; and a trust in God in the way of sin is what is called presumption, which is a thing terribly threatened in His Word.

JONATHAN EDWARDS

PRIDE

Let us not be turned aside nor drawn away by ambition or vainglory.

Nothing is more contrary to faith than pride, as also humility is the principle of faith.

Pride is always the companion of unbelief.

[God] denominates all unbelievers proud (*Psa.* 119:21) because it is true faith alone which humbles us and all rebellion is the offspring of pride.

JOHN CALVIN

PRIDE

Alas! that idol *myself* is the master-idol we all bow to.

SAMUEL RUTHERFORD

Humility is part of the image of God; pride is the masterpiece of the image of the devil.

Humility and lowliness of spirit qualify us for friendly communion with God in Christ. Pride makes God our enemy (*1 Pet.* 5:5).

THOMAS BOSTON

PROMISES

At preaching of the law men repent, and at preaching of the promises they believe.

WILLIAM TYNDALE

The hope of the promise can put up with everything . . . We are all sustained by the Word of God.

The entire Scripture of God is divided into two parts, commandments and promises . . . The promises of God give what the commandments of God demand, and fulfil what the law preaches.

MARTIN LUTHER

What benefit do God's promises confer on us, unless we embrace them by faith?

If one promise of God be not enough for us, let us go to another, and so forth, to a third . . . so as the seed of unbelief may be utterly rooted out of our hearts.

There is no place for faith if we expect God to fulfil immediately what He promises. It is the trial of faith to acquiesce in God's Word. We have no faith except we are satisfied with God's Word alone.

This is the true proof of faith, when we never suffer ourselves to be torn away from Christ, and from the promises.

It is the Word of God alone which can first and effectually check the heart of the sinner. There is no true or solid peace to be enjoyed in the world except in the way of reposing upon the promises of God.

It is no light matter to give credit to the promises of God, and to hold to them.

Nothing does more hinder or prevent us from embracing the promises of God, than to think of what may be done naturally, or of what is probable. When we thus consult our own thoughts, we exclude the power of God.

His promises are always of no avail until He prints them in our hearts; this He does by His Holy Spirit.

We may well apply to ourselves all the promises that are given in the Holy Scriptures . . . not so much as one mite of them shall fail.

We are not qualified for enjoying the promises of God, unless we have received the remission of sins . . . The promise by which God adopts us to Himself as His Sons, holds the first place among them all.

Faith cannot stand unless it be founded upon the promises of God.

Our faith should be borne up on wings by the promises of God.

God shall sooner renounce Himself than not perform His promises.

All the promises which are possible to be wished, were given of God unto Abraham before he had showed any sign of faith or of the fear of God.

Not by taking some small taste of God's promises, as it were at a glance only, but by setting our minds upon them, and by exercising ourselves daily in them.

The end and use of promises is to excite us to prayer.

As soon as we cease to be aware of the promises of God we fail.

There are promises that belong but to the present life, and we see not those promises performed always after one rate, but as God knows them to be expedient for us. As touching the spiritual promises that belong to the welfare of our souls; they are certain . . . God will never disappoint us of them.

The design of all God's promises . . . to keep us from being disturbed, to give us quietness of mind, and to cause us to look for the help promised to us.

Had I been the servant of men I had obtained a poor reward, but it is well that I have served Him who never fails to perform to His servants whatever He has promised.

JOHN CALVIN

Faith looks on the omnipotency of God joined with His promises.

JOHN BRADFORD

God never out-promised Himself.

The most valuable of all the promises was the longest in fulfilment, viz. the promise of Christ – 4000 years.

The glory of all God's attributes is engaged for the performance of His promises.

THOMAS BOSTON

PROPHECY – OLD TESTAMENT

All prophecy before the coming of the Lord is a lamp . . . The prophets are lamps, and all prophecy one great lamp.

AUGUSTINE

God restored all the prophecies in our Lord Jesus Christ which had, as it were, been broken off for a time.

JOHN CALVIN

PROPHECY – OLD TESTAMENT
(Continued)

The strongest proofs of the Messiahship of Jesus are taken from prophecy . . . a standing miracle from the commencement of the church to the end of time.

BLAISE PASCAL

PROPHETS

God sets prophets in opposition to soothsayers, diviners, foretellers, and all other ministers of Satan.

JOHN CALVIN

God never more honoured His true prophets than when there were false ones.

JOHN OWEN

PROPITIATION

Let no one be misled . . . if they fail to believe in Christ's blood, they too are doomed.

IGNATIUS

Since this is a thing that is beyond the reach of the human mind, let us who have ever truly sought after God learn, under the guidance and teaching of Scripture, that He appointed the propitiation to be by blood.

JOHN CALVIN

Propitiation properly means the turning away of wrath by an offering . . . The idea of the wrath of God is stubbornly rooted in the Old Testament, where it is referred to 585 times . . . The paradox of the Old Testament is repeated in the New, that God Himself provides the means of removing His own wrath . . . The sin of man has incurred the wrath of God. That wrath is averted only by Christ's atoning sacrifice.

LEON MORRIS

The idea of propitiation is so woven into the fabric of Old Testament ritual that it would be impossible to regard that ritual as the pattern of the sacrifice of Christ if propitiation did not occupy a similar place in the one great sacrifice offered.

JOHN MURRAY

PROVIDENCE

God still reigns though it is after a dark manner.

God's judgments are not ruled by man's discretion, but are secret and hidden from us.

If the devil were not held in control and all the wicked were not governed by the counsel and the secret and incomprehensible power of God, where would we be?

Except God governs the world there is no salvation to the faithful.

It is the property of God to bring the counsels of men to nought.

We see now after what sort we must consider God's providence, namely . . . that nothing may be done which He has not determined so as His will is the rule of all things . . . It behoves us to mind well the providence of God . . . that when adversity befalls us, we may always go to the first cause.

Our Lord works in such wise that He turns darkness into light, and deadly poison to our health.

Our Lord will not use might without right.

JOHN CALVIN

How grand it is to see, by the eye of faith, Darius and Cyrus, Alexander, the Roman Pompey and Herod working, though unconsciously, for the glory of the gospel.

BLAISE PASCAL

God's directing and commanding will can by no good logic be concluded from events of Providence.

God can make one web of contraries.

SAMUEL RUTHERFORD

PSALMS/PSALMODY

Whoever wants to arouse himself to devotion, should take up the Psalms.

MARTIN LUTHER

The same songs, which were then only heard in Judea, would resound in every quarter of the globe.

JOHN CALVIN

The solution that made possible genuine and nearly universal congregational participation in the Reformed Churches was metrical psalmody.

The Metrical Psalter became the most powerful proselytizing instrument of the Reformation.

ANON.

The Venerable Bede, when approaching his death, AD 735, 'gave daily lessons to his students and spent the rest of the day in singing the Psalms . . . and [an eyewitness said] I have never heard anyone who gave thanks so unceasingly as he'.

[On Psalm 22]. Loaded with the sins of the world, Jesus began the Psalm upon the cross to show it was His. Four out of the last seven words [on the cross] are taken from or refer to it.

WILLIAM ALEXANDER

REASON

The authority [of Scripture] does not fix a limit on reason; it asserts the existence of a limit already fixed in the constitution of our nature.

JOHN DUNCAN

REDEMPTION

Except by this way no man has been delivered, no man is delivered, no man shall be delivered.

AUGUSTINE

I expect, with Paul, a reparation of all the evils caused by sin.

Redemption is the first gift of Christ that is begun in us, and the last that is completed (*Rom.*8:23).

JOHN CALVIN

The fundamental characteristic of the New Testament conception of redemption is that deliverance from guilt stands first; emancipation from the power of sin follows upon it; and removal of all the ills of life constitute the final issue.

O. KIRN

Redemption denotes the means by which salvation is achieved,namely, the payment of a ransom.

EVERETT F. HARRISON

Redemption in biblical thought is always redemption from slavery, either the slavery of Egypt and Babylon or the slavery of sin.

R. V. G. TASKER

REGENERATION

In the new birth man receives back the Spirit of God which at the beginning he received from God's inbreathing, but which he after-

wards lost through his transgression.

TERTULLIAN

The grace of regeneration was promised to the ancient people when God consecrated the seventh day. The Sabbath was a sacrament — a visible word.

We have nothing of the Spirit except by regeneration.

JOHN CALVIN

The same overshadowing power which formed His [Christ's] human nature, re-forms ours . . . He who was born for us upon His incarnation, is born within us upon our regeneration.

JOHN PEARSON, quoting JEROME

The true reason why any despise the new birth is that they hate a new life.

The work of the Holy Spirit in regeneration does not consist in raptures, ecstasies, visions, enthusiastic inspirations, but in the effect of the power of the Holy Spirit of God on the souls of men, by and according to His Word.

JOHN OWEN

In regeneration the will is cured of its utter inability to will what is good; there is wrought a fixed aversion to evil, the will is endowed with an inclination, bent and propensity to good; it is conformed to God's preceptive will, being endowed with holy inclinations agreeable to every one of His commands. The whole law is impressed upon the gracious soul.

THOMAS BOSTON

In man exists what is human; in the new man what is divine.

J. A. BENGEL

[In regeneration] 1. A principle of holiness is implanted. 2. Spiritual life is communicated. 3. The mind is enlightened. 4. The will is renewed. 5. The affections are elevated.

ARCHIBALD ALEXANDER

Though we are passive in our regeneration we are not to be passive about it or after it.

JOHN DUNCAN

The loss of the Spirit, and the restoration of the Spirit . . . are the two most momentous facts in the history of man.

GEORGE SMEATON

The characteristic of all Pharisaism is that it ignores and fights regeneration.

ERNST HENGSTENBERG

Spiritual birth is something one undergoes, not something he produces.

R.C.H. LENSKI

REPENTANCE

Repentance brings true humility.

It is the ordinary practice of Scripture, whenever redemption is mentioned, to exhort us to repentance.

The beginning of repentance is the confession of guilt.

Repentance . . . the peculiar gift of God . . . God is not called the Helper in repentance but the Author of it.

Repentance . . . an inward turning to God which shows itself afterwards by external works.

Repentance throws men downwards, and faith raises them upwards again.

Repentance, if it is true and sincere, will never be too late.

Men cannot be led to repentance in any other way than by holding out assurance of pardon.

True repentance is firm and constant, and makes us war with the evil that is in us, not for a day, or a week, but without end and without intermission.

Repentance does not consist in one or two words, but in perseverance.

False prophets . . . speak only of God's freeness to forgive, and are profoundly silent about repentance.

Affliction is the true schoolmistress to bring men to repentance.

JOHN CALVIN

REPENTANCE
(CONTINUED)

The doctrine of repentance is an odious one for us, and we would prefer it practically never to be brought up.

Faith . . . cannot exist without repentance.

JOHN CALVIN

All true and saving repentance tends to holy practice.

JONATHAN EDWARDS

Repentance is in every way so desirable, so necessary, so suited to honour God, that I seek that above all.

CHARLES SIMEON

All true repentance springs from right views of God. It destroys the disposition to self-justification.

The call to repentance follows men from the cradle to the grave.

Every command to repent implies a readiness on the part of God to forgive.

Faith and repentance cannot exist separately. Repentance is the act of a believer; and faith is the act of a penitent; so that whoever believes repents; and whoever repents believes.

The repentance of the ungodly, consists in the operations of conscience combined with fear; the repentance of the godly, of the operations of conscience combined with love.

CHARLES HODGE

A change of mind respecting God, respecting ourselves, respecting sin and respecting righteousness.

JOHN MURRAY

REPROOF

If a man should speak to the people of Geneva nowadays as Moses spoke to the people of Israel, and reprove folks' sins, as they deserve, should he be received?

JOHN CALVIN

RESPONSIBILITY

All whom God does not enlighten with the Spirit of adoption are men of unsound mind; and while they are more and more blinded by the Word of God, the blame rests wholly on themselves, because this blindness is voluntary.

As no man is excluded from calling upon God, the gate of salvation is set open to all men, neither is there anything which keeps us back from entering in, save only our unbelief.

God holds the impious under His guidance as it were, for executing His judgments; but God has a method, wonderful and incomprehensible to us, which impels them hither and thither, so that He does not involve Himself in any alliance with their fault.

JOHN CALVIN

[On God's Sovereignty and man's responsibility] The true object is gained . . . by exhibiting the two sides of the incomprehensible mystery. They are both true; and all that theology effects is to conserve the mystery.

GEORGE SMEATON

The act of regeneration does not come within the sphere of our responsible action. Faith does. And we are never relieved of the obligation to believe in Christ to the saving of our souls. The fact that regeneration is the prerequisite of faith in no way relieves us of the responsibility to believe. Our inability is no excuse for our unbelief nor does it provide us with any reason for not believing.

JOHN MURRAY

Predestination and free agency are the twin pillars of a great temple, and they meet above the clouds where the human gaze cannot penetrate.

LORAINE BOETTNER

RESURRECTION

The bodies of the saints shall, after the resurrection, be spiritual, and yet flesh shall not be changed into spirit.

After the resurrection, the body, having become wholly subject to the spirit, will live in perfect peace to all eternity.

The only reason why [Christ] came is in order that souls may have a resurrection from iniquity, and bodies from corruption.

Greater is the resurrection of the body unto eternity than this healing of the body.

AUGUSTINE

He ascended not into heaven to leave us here beneath to rot in our furrows, but to open us the gate, and by taking possession in our name, to gather us to Him.

The resurrection at the last day . . . surpasses all other miracles.

God watches over the scattered dust of His own children, gathers it again, and will suffer nothing of them to perish.

It was a dangerous thing to scoff when they insinuated doubt as to the last resurrection; for when that is taken away, there is no gospel any longer, the power of Christ is brought to nothing, the whole of religion is gone.

JOHN CALVIN

The belief of this Article [of resurrection] serves to strengthen us against the fear of our own death, and to moderate sorrow for the death of others . . . This encourages all drooping spirits, this sustains all fainting hearts, this sweetens all present miseries, this lightens all heavy burdens, this

RESURRECTION
(CONTINUED)

encourages in all dangers, this supports in all calamities.

JOHN PEARSON

Q: What benefits do believers receive from Christ at the resurrection?
A: At the resurrection, believers being raised up in glory, shall be openly acknowledged and acquitted in the day of judgment, and made perfectly blessed in the full enjoying of God to all eternity.

WESTMINSTER SHORTER CATECHISM, *Question and Answer 38*

The victory which was death's is now ours . . . Victory in an open court of law, the high court of heaven.

The union of believers to Christ is the explanation of the connection between his resurrection and theirs . . . Their resurrection is the complement of His own.

ROBERT CANDLISH

The moral significance of such a doctrine as the Resurrection of the body cannot be overrated.

BROOKE FOSS WESCOTT

In the Bible 'resurrection', in opposition to Hellenism, must be resurrection of the body.

OSCAR CULLMANN

REVERENCE

Faith is always connected with a seemly and spontaneous reverence for God.

JOHN CALVIN

Reverence is the sense of truth, put in practice.

HENRY LIDDON

ROMAN CATHOLICISM

The Roman Catholic has to earn heaven for himself.

W. NIESEL

All the Papists think themselves to be saved by keeping the law: and I myself have been of that dangerous and damnable opinion till I was thirty years of age. So long I walked in darkness.

Let us keep ourselves within the hedges of God's holy Word . . . In God's Word we shall stand fast, but not in Popery.

HUGH LATIMER

The Papacy is a horrible abyss; for no one under that system can have a firm footing.

JOHN CALVIN

The Mass . . . a disannulling of Christ's death.

JOHN KNOX

The Roman Catholic Council of Trent on the Mass: That same Christ is contained and immolated in an unbloody manner on the altar of the cross; and this sacrifice is truly propitiatory.

THE SABBATH [1]

The Pharisees kept the Sabbath carnally and profaned it spiritually.

The first distinct mention of sanctification in the law of God was on the seventh day [Gen. 2:3].

AUGUSTINE

Now we be no more tied to the old bondage of keeping the Sabbath day . . . We be no more bound to the ceremony that was kept so straitly under the Law.

So much as concerns the order continues still and has its use . . . We must refrain from our own business. We must call upon His Name and exercise ourselves in His Word . . . to be taught together to make confession of our faith and to exercise ourselves in the use of the sacraments.

JOHN CALVIN

In keeping of some Festival days our Church consented not; for only the Sabbath day was kept in Scotland.

JOHN KNOX

Q: Which day of the seven has God appointed to be the weekly Sabbath? A: From the beginning of the world to the resurrection of Christ, God

[1] See also THE LORD'S DAY

appointed the seventh day of the week to be the weekly Sabbath; and the first day of the week ever since, to continue to the end of the world, is the Christian Sabbath.

WESTMINSTER SHORTER CATECHISM, *Question and Answer 59*

The Sabbath: this precious fence which the goodness of God has drawn around the vineyard of his church.

JOHN OWEN

How dull the Sabbath day
Without the Sabbath's Lord!
How toilsome then to sing and pray
And wait upon the Word!

WILLIAM COWPER

Unlike the others of the Ten Commandments the Sabbath law has in it two elements: the moral and the ceremonial . . . The Sabbath law was not one merely of rest, but of rest for worship. The service of the Lord was the object in view.

ALFRED EDERSHEIM

THE SACRAMENTS

The first object of [the sacraments] is to assist our faith towards God, the second, to testify our confession before men.

What is a sacrament taken without faith, but the certain ruin of the Church?

Everyone receives from the sign just as much benefit as his vessel of faith can contain.

THE SABBATH
(Continued)

Whatever grace is communicated to us by the Sacraments is to be ascribed to faith. He who separates faith from the Sacraments does just as if he were to take the soul away from the body.

The device of *opus operandum* is recent, and was coined by illiterate monks . . . In the Sacraments God alone properly acts; men bring nothing of their own.

If the Word is taken away the whole power of the sacraments is gone.

JOHN CALVIN

SALVATION

Man cannot save himself; cannot even begin to save himself; nor of himself even begin to hope for salvation.

AUGUSTINE

A man cannot be thoroughly humbled until he comes to know that his salvation is utterly beyond his own powers, counsel, endeavours, will and works, and absolutely depending on the will, counsel, pleasure and work of another . . . God only.

MARTIN LUTHER

There is nothing necessary for salvation which faith finds not in Christ.

JOHN CALVIN

Salvation is 'to' as well as 'from'.

JOHN MURRAY

I always thought that Jesus Christ came to save saints; and when I saw that He came to save sinners I wept for joy.

A SEEKING WOMAN, to ALEXANDER
MOODY STUART

Paul always deals with salvation as a whole. He sees it from the beginning right to the end.

D. MARTYN LLOYD-JONES

SANCTIFICATION

There is no motive to a holy life so powerful and efficacious as that which is drawn from the propitiatory work of Christ.

Everyone's advancement in piety is the secret work of the Holy Spirit.

JOHN CALVIN

[Sanctification] gives saving light in the mind, and life in the will, and love in the affections, and grace in the conscience.

Sanctification is the universal renovation of our natures by the Holy Spirit into the image of God, through Jesus Christ.

Our love to Christ is the principal part of our renovation to His image. Nothing renders us so like unto God as our love unto Jesus Christ.

Every believer is truly and really sanctified at once, but none is perfectly sanctified at once.

In the sanctification of believers, the Holy Spirit works in them, in their whole soul, their minds, wills and affections a gracious supernatural habit, principle and disposition of living unto God.

JOHN OWEN

The Puritans were raised up to give the same prominence to Sanctification as Martin Luther had given to Justification.

JAMES BUCHANAN

You will notice that those who make most of the Word of God make most progress in the divine life.

HORATIUS BONAR

I am more than ever convinced that sanctification is carried on by the Spirit by means of our direct looking on the face of Jesus hour by hour.

ANDREW BONAR

Sanctification is placed in direct and immediate relation to the atonement.

GEORGE SMEATON

God has ordered our sanctification to flow from Christ directly. The Holy Spirit is the worker yet whatever He imparts to us He takes from Christ.

It wounds the very heart of the Reformed confession when the pulpit aims at sanctification without zeal for justification.

ABRAHAM KUYPER

The Reformers represented the Christian life as a life of continuous dissatisfaction with self, and of continuous looking afresh to Christ as the ground of all our hope.

B. B. WARFIELD

The process of sanctification is transformation into the image of Christ (*2 Cor.* 3:18) . . . This does not take place by quiescent passivity on our part. It is only by concentrated application to the data of revelation that we come into this encounter with the glory of the Lord. And all the energies of our being are enlisted in the exercise of adoration, love, obedience and fellowship.

The dynamic in sanctification is the virtue proceeding from the glorified Christ.

JOHN MURRAY

A deep sense of duty is the greatest thing in the moral life of the Calvinist.

LORAINE BOETTNER

SATAN

Satan we call the angel of evil, the contriver of all error, the corrupter of the whole world.

TERTULLIAN

SATAN
(Continued)

The whole world . . . is subject to the Creator, not to the deserter; to the Redeemer, not to the destroyer; to the Deliverer; not to the enslaver; to the Teacher, not to the deceiver.

Nor is there any middle place for any man, so that a man can only be with the devil who is not with Christ.

The devil, as a solace for his own damnation, seeks others whose companionship he may obtain in that damnation.

God uses our worst enemy, the devil . . . to exercise the faith and piety of good men.

AUGUSTINE

[On Psa. 77:20] Faith understands that the devil has been conquered, death killed, and heaven opened; but reason does not know it.

MARTIN LUTHER

The devil beareth himself in hand to be lord and ruler over the whole world: but in very deed he hath not so much as a goose-feather by right.

HUGH LATIMER

Satan . . . an ape who always counterfeits God's works.

The whole of Satan's kingdom is subject to the authority of Christ.

It is customary with Satan to exaggerate in words the power of the enemies and to represent the dangers as greater than they are.

It has been God's will in all ages to try the faith of His servants by permitting to Satan and his ministers the liberty of pretending falsely His holy name.

What a subtle contriver Satan is! — to turn us aside under the cover of zeal from the course of our vocation. Beware of the intrigues of Satan . . . for we see that some leave the church because they require in it the highest perfection . . . and seek to form for themselves a new world in which there is to be a perfect church . . . They depart from God Himself, and violate the unity of the church.

If we contend with Satan according to our own view of things, he will a hundred times overwhelm us and we will never be able to resist.

No other reason can be assigned why the fury of Satan meets with so little resistance, and why so many are everywhere carried away by him, but that God punishes their carelessness and their contempt of His Word.

Because Satan could not drag God from His throne he assailed man, in whom His image shone. He endeavoured, in the person of man, to obscure the glory of God.

Let us look at Satan and all our spiritual enemies as already vanquished, and assure ourselves beforehand that God will make us to triumph in the midst of our battles.

The devil has used the name of God throughout the ages as a cloak to cover his lies, and disguise them as truth.

Satan could not give us a more deadly wound than by corrupting the sincerity of the gospel, for therein stands our hope.

Satan . . . practises all he can against us to cast us into despair.

The devil presents us with many opportunities to grow cold.

God allows more power and liberty to Satan over wicked and ungodly ministers, than over ordinary men.

We see the devil's subtlety, who desires nothing so much as that the churches should be destitute of good shepherds.

When anyone begins to rely on God, he must lay his account with and arm himself for sustaining many assaults from Satan.

The worst men are in God's hand as Satan is who is their head. Who is the prince of strife but the devil?

The devil has troubled the church, sowing error by masking his activity in the name of God; and the only way to overcome him is by keeping to the Word of God in its entirety.

The devil strives ceaselessly to turn us to evil . . . and to entangle us in new curiosities.

The devil has many demons who are seeking to throw everything into confusion today, and whose sole employment is the suppression of the Christian faith.

Even the devil can sometimes act as a doctor for us.

The devil has his martyrs.

The devil by his artifice fascinates the reprobate when he renders God's Word either hateful or contemptible.

JOHN CALVIN

The devil chiefly desires his seat to be in religion.

JOHN BRADFORD

It is easy for God to make a fool of the devil, the father of all fools.

Antichrist biteth the sorest when he bleedeth the fastest.

SAMUEL RUTHERFORD

The devil is a greater scholar than you, and a nimbler disputant . . . He will play the juggler with you undiscerned.

RICHARD BAXTER

SATAN
(Continued)

Satan is not so poor a politician as to be without his agents in our ecclesiastical armies.

RICHARD BAXTER

Satan's sin consisted of two parts: 1. His pride against the Person of the Son of God, by whom he was created (*Col.* 1:16). 2. Envy against mankind, made in the image of God, of the Son of God, the first-born.

It has been the desire of Satan, in all ages, to contrive presumptuous notions of men's spiritual abilities.

Man, by sin, put himself into the power of the devil, God's greatest adversary.

JOHN OWEN

Satan makes choice of persons of place and power. These are either in the Commonwealth or Church. If he can he will secure the throne and the pulpit, as the two forts that command the whole line.

Satan leads poor creatures down into the depths of sin by winding stairs, that let them not see the bottom whither they are going.

WILLIAM GURNALL

'Ye shall not surely die' – the first article of the devil's creed.

THOMAS BOSTON

There are other spirits who have influence on the minds of men besides the Holy Spirit.

JONATHAN EDWARDS

In Genesis 3 we have the methods of Satan. In Job 1 we have the tactics of Satan. In Matthew 4 we have the most subtle strategy of Satan.

ADOLPH SAPHIR

THE SCHOOL OF GOD

As long as we are in this world we are in God's school.

Our wisdom to be learners to the end.

No person can serve God aright but he has been taught in His school.

The Scripture is the school of the Holy Spirit, in which, as nothing necessary and useful to be known is omitted, so nothing is taught which it is not beneficial to know.

JOHN CALVIN

All along Christ has taught men gradually . . . Until our last day God is teaching us.

HENRY LIDDON

SEPARATION FROM THE WORLD

When the lovers of the world revile us, let us say to them, 'Your time is always ready; our time is not yet come.'

AUGUSTINE

If you were not strangers here, the dogs of the world would not bark at you.

SAMUEL RUTHERFORD

The main end of the holy Word of God is to untie the hearts of men from the world, and to reduce them to God.

ROBERT LEIGHTON

Christ is little esteemed by us when the admiration of worldly glory lays hold of us.

We cannot have the company of Jesus Christ unless we be as wayfarers in this world.

By the power of the Holy Spirit we are able to forsake the world and ourselves.

God will not take us to heaven, into the vision and possession of heavenly glory, with our heads and hearts reeking with the thoughts and affections of earthly things.

JOHN OWEN

Thousands have been hugged to death in the embraces of a smiling world.

THOMAS BOSTON

SEPARATION FROM THE CHURCH

The sole cause of our secession has been that theirs cannot possibly be the pure profession of the truth.

Sinners, even hypocrites, must be tolerated in the Church, but not those who propagate false doctrine.

God's sacred barn-floor will not be properly cleansed before the last day.

Although it may not be in our power to cleanse the Church of God, it is our duty to desire her purity.

JOHN CALVIN

We must abhor the arrogancy of them that frame engines to harass and tear the Church of God under pretence of obviating errors and maintaining the truth.

RICHARD BAXTER

For parties to separate wantonly and on insufficient grounds from the communion of the visible Church, is a grave and serious offence against the authority of Christ in His house.

JAMES BANNERMAN

Perfectionists swarmed over the land, drawing from all churches, forming none.

B. B. WARFIELD

As long as [a believer] is not compelled to say or do something which his conscience, based on the Word of God, would forbid, he ought to remain in the church and obey her discipline.

AUGUSTE LECERF

SEPARATION
FROM ERROR

With reference to Gilbert Tennent's sermon *The Danger of an Unconverted Ministry*, George Whitefield noted: 'God does not require men to starve their own souls by hearing such preachers.'

SERMONS

When we come to a sermon, or when we take the Bible in our hands to read, God cites and summons us . . . His majesty is present therewith, and we are present in His sight.

JOHN CALVIN

Care should be taken on the choice of texts, proofs and quotations from the Scripture, to ascertain not only what is said, but also to whom it was said.

ABRAHAM KUYPER

SICKNESS

Do not attribute the effects of mere disease to the devil.

ARCHIBALD ALEXANDER

Envy, fear, hate, when these sentiments are habitual, are capable of starting organic changes and genuine diseases. Moral suffering profoundly disturbs health.

In sickness the body preserves the same unity as in health. It is sick as a whole, no disturbance remains strictly confined to a single organ.

ALEXIS CARRELL

SIN

The eye of my soul has been damaged by my sins.

The knowledge of the law — through which comes the discovery, not the expulsion of sin.

The vast majority of men . . . are swifter to make excuses for their sins than to make confession of them.

The man who despises the mercy of God is guilty of the sin against the Holy Ghost.

AUGUSTINE

Of the enormity of sin no man was ever convinced but by the Holy Spirit Himself.

MARTIN LUTHER

That platonic dogma is false, that ignorance alone is the cause of sin.

If God should discover our secret faults (*Psa.* 19:12), there would be found in us an abyss of sins so great as to have neither bottom nor shore.

There will always be spots and stains within us, and we will always be bent down with the burden of our sins and weaknesses . . . Our life is to be a constant battle.

We throw heaven and earth into confusion by our sins: for were we in a right order as to our obedience to God, doubtless all the elements would be conformable, and we should thus observe in the world an angelic harmony.

Men are attainted with the vice of hypocrisy . . . Adam began first that trade, and showed the same to all who came of his race . . . All of us have it by nature.

Why know we not the greatness of our sins? Because we tie scarves before our eyes.

It is always profitable that the sense of sin should remain.

There still remains in a regenerate man a fountain of evil, continually producing irregular desires . . . This warfare will be terminated only by death.

The contempt of His Word ever led [Israel] to sin (*Heb.* 3:17).

JOHN CALVIN

New washing, renewed application of purchased redemption, by that sacred blood which sealeth the free covenant, is a thing of daily and hourly use to a poor sinner.

The more sense of sin, the less sin.

SAMUEL RUTHERFORD

He that falls into sin is a man; that grieves at it is a saint; that boasts of it is a devil.

Samson's hair grew again, but not his eyes. Time may restore some losses, others are never repaired.

THOMAS FULLER

This principle of sin, however it may be dethroned, corrected, impaired and disabled, yet is it never wholly and absolutely dispossessed and cast out of the soul in this life.

It is sin only that makes a Saviour necessary.

Unbelief has more malignity in it than all other sins.

JOHN OWEN

We run carelessly to the precipice, after having veiled our eyes to hinder us from seeing it.

BLAISE PASCAL

It has been my every day's portion to be let into the evil of my own heart.

JOHN BUNYAN

The stately ruins are visible to every eye, that bear in their front yet extant this doleful inscription: *Here God once dwelt.*

JOHN HOWE

Our liberty and prosperity depend upon Reformation. Make it a shame to see men bold in sin and profaneness, and God will bless you.

OLIVER CROMWELL'S speech to the English Parliament, 17 September 1656.

SIN
(Continued)

It is as natural for us to hide sin as to commit it. Who of Adam's sons needs to be taught how to sew fig leaves together?

My heart-monsters, pride, worldly-mindedness, discontent, stared me in the face.

Shame follows sin as the shadow the body.

Sin vilifies the wisdom of God.

THOMAS BOSTON

He that has not willed that sin and he should part, cannot have willed to receive Christ as His Saviour to part them.

Sin is like some distempers of the eyes that make things to appear of different colours from those which properly belong to them.

JONATHAN EDWARDS

The words crime and criminal belong to every language; but sin and sinner belong exclusively to the vocabulary of Christian revelation.

JOSEPH DE MAISTRE

Sinning is not a rare thing, but repenting is; sinning not rare, but taking a right view of sin, saying right about sin, that is rare.

If one sin destroyed man's moral nature, every sin strengthens man's depravity.

JOHN DUNCAN

A sense of personal unworthiness is the principal part of conviction of sin . . . This includes a conviction of our condemnation before God . . . the touchstone of a true conversion.

CHARLES HODGE

Unhappiness is inseparable from sin, and should bear an exact proportion to it . . . Sorrow and sin seek each other out.

ALEXANDRE VINET

[On the sins of saints] 1. Want of faith, 2. Want of humility, 3. Want of love (Rev. 2:1–4), 4. Want of unity or harmony.

ROBERT MURRAY M'CHEYNE

Opposition to the will of God destroys our liberty, 'and he that commits sin is the servant of sin'.

CHRISTOPH LUTHARDT

To understand the nature of sin we must depth three oceans:
1. The ocean of human suffering,
2. The ocean of Christ's suffering,
3. The ocean of future suffering.

HENRY GRATTAN GUINNESS

The theory that sin is a mere loss, default or lack is an error.

Man could not sin so terribly if God had not created him after His own image.

From sin proceed guilt, penalty and stain. From these three we must be delivered. From the penalty by

Christ's atonement; from guilt by His satisfaction, and from the stain by sanctification.

Scripture teaches that sin does not originate in the flesh, but in Satan, a being without a body. Coming from him it crept first into man's soul, then manifested itself in the body.

ABRAHAM KUYPER

Without [the fact of the Fall] man's sin would remain an unsolved riddle.

JAMES ORR

To be a sinner means to be engaged in rebellion against God.

The false understanding of freedom is the very quintessence of sin. Sin is the desire for freedom and the illusion that it is possible to be free from God.

EMIL BRUNNER

We may find a great deal of emphasis upon the undesirability of sin, the odiousness, ugliness, even filthiness of sin, without any truly Christian assessment of sin as lawlessness, pollution and guilt.

JOHN MURRAY

Nothing short of an infinite sacrifice for sin is an adequate declaration of the infinite abhorrence with which sin is regarded by a Being of infinite purity.

J. T. O'BRIEN

SLANDER

As long as we hear them evil spoken of that preach the Word of God, let us suspect the devil, for slanders come always out of his shop.

The best servers of God shall be slandered and wronged.

JOHN CALVIN

Satan slanders us . . . the Protestants of the Realme of Scotland seek nothing but Christ Jesus in His glorious Evangel to be preached.

JOHN KNOX

THE SOVEREIGNTY OF GOD

Sovereignty is a relation, more especially a justice relation. Over against man [God] has only rights, no duties: man, on the other hand, has only duties towards Him, but can lay claim to not a single right against Him.

EVANGELICAL QUARTERLY, 1932

The will of God is never defeated, though much is done that is contrary to His will . . . Even what is done in opposition to His will does not defeat His will.

Men's wills cannot withstand the will of God.

AUGUSTINE

All our adversities are turned to our welfare.

JOHN CALVIN

THE SOVEREIGNTY OF GOD

(CONTINUED)

No difficulties can prevent the Lord from delivering and restoring His church whenever He shall think fit.

The life and death of every king and nation are in the hand and at the will of God.

JOHN CALVIN

[*Concerning the time of persecution under Mary Tudor*] Look not upon these days . . . as dismal days and days of God's vengeance, but rather as lucky days and days of God's fatherly kindness toward us.

JOHN BRADFORD

The Lord hath a way whereby He will be the only reaper of praises.

SAMUEL RUTHERFORD

The sovereignty of God and the responsibility of man were two doctrines which the Haldanes never tried to reconcile, but both of which they fully and strongly taught.

ALEXANDER HALDANE

God alone has the right to determine what is good or evil.

ABRAHAM KUYPER

STUDY

The holiest men in the Christian church have been the most studious. God bestows a blessing on intellectual seriousness.

MARTIN LUTHER

SUFFERING

In Christ sufferings are salutary . . . Faith causes sufferings to be useful and injuries to be pleasant.

MARTIN LUTHER

We see different persons exercised with different kinds of crosses. But whilst the heavenly Physician, consulting the health of all His patients, practises a milder treatment towards some, and cures others with rougher remedies, yet He leaves no one completely exempted, because He knows we are all diseased, without the exception of a single individual.

JOHN CALVIN

I hang by a thread, but it is of Christ's spinning. There is no quarrel more honest or honourable than to suffer for truth.

Suffering is the other half of our ministry, albeit the hardest.

SAMUEL RUTHERFORD.

TEMPTATION

There are two kinds of temptation, the one that deceives, the other, that proves.

AUGUSTINE

The greatest temptation of all is to have no temptation.

Do not argue with the devil and his temptations and accusations and arguments, nor, by the example of Christ refute them. Just keep silent altogether; turn away and hold him in contempt.

MARTIN LUTHER

There is a great difference between being utterly beaten down by a temptation, and the feeling of it.

When God gives Satan leave to tempt the faithful, ordinarily it is to make them to be served as with a medicine. Herein we see God's marvellous goodness, how He turns the evil into good.

Whenever Satan assails us let us understand that God is minded to exercise us.

[*Of Satan's tempting of Christ*] The single object Satan has in view is to persuade Christ to depart from the Word of God.

Of all the battles that we have to fight against, the temptations of our flesh, the greatest . . . is against unbelief, and specially when we feel any of God's chastisements.

JOHN CALVIN.

The devil is but God's master fencer to teach us to handle our weapons.

SAMUEL RUTHERFORD

Three means of destruction [of the town of Mansoul] are proposed in hell: (1) A vicious life (2) Despair of mercy (3) Prevailing pride.

JOHN BUNYAN

Satan fell to his old trade, and snarled like a dog at my heels, and it did me good.

THOMAS BOSTON

It is dangerous to gather flowers that grow on the banks of the pit of hell. They who play with the devil's rattles will be brought by degrees to wield his sword.

THOMAS FULLER

TESTIMONY

And I profess before God and His holy angels that I never made gain of the sacred Word of God; that I never studied to please men, never indulged my own private passions, or those of others, but faithfully distributed the talent entrusted to my care for the edification of the church over which I did watch.

JOHN KNOX

THE TRINITY

This truth is too difficult to command the assent of the human mind.

JOHN CALVIN

There are three persons in the Godhead, the Father, the Son, and the Holy Ghost; and these three are one God, the same in substance, equal in power and glory.

WESTMINSTER SHORTER CATECHISM, *Answer 6*

THE TRINITY
(Continued)

There was no more glorious mystery brought to light in and by Jesus Christ than that of the holy Trinity, or the subsistence of the three Persons in the unity of the same divine nature.

JOHN OWEN

The unity of the Godhead required that as the extent of the Father's gift, and the extent of the sanctifying work of the Holy Spirit, such also must be the extent of the atonement or reconciliation effected by the Son.

JAMES HALDANE

TROUBLE

All our troubles grow on this root of an over-valuation of temporal things . . . The mind on all such occasions is its own greatest trouble.

JOHN OWEN

TRUST

Reach out your trust to the uttermost.

We put our trust in Him, and stick to His promises, not doubting but that He will give things a good end, though they seem utterly past all hope.

JOHN CALVIN

TRUTH

Truth is more powerful than eloquence . . . The victory is in the hands of children speaking truth, not in the hands of lying eloquence.

MARTIN LUTHER

Nothing can give me pain which I shall suffer in defence of truth.

HUGH LATIMER, quoting JEROME

His truth will be so mighty that in the end it will get the upper hand.

JOHN CALVIN

All truths are not alike clear, alike necessary, nor of like concernment to every one. Christians should keep within their line.

ROBERT LEIGHTON

We make an ill use of the opportunity God grants us of suffering for the establishment of truth . . . We act as if commissioned to ensure the triumph of truth, instead of being only appointed to fight for it.

We can enter into the truth only by love.

God alone can put [divine truths] into the soul . . . He chooses that they should pass from the heart into the understanding, and not from the understanding into the heart, in order to humble that proud faculty of reason.

BLAISE PASCAL

He alone *understands* divine truth who *does* it.

JOHN OWEN

Be sure you have the truth and then be sure you hold it.

CHARLES H. SPURGEON

All truth is known to be truth by its tendency to promote holiness.

CHARLES HODGE

It is not entertainment we need. It is truth. It is knowledge. It is the doctrines of this great epistle [Romans] and of the other epistles. It is as we know and really have appropriated them, that we shall be stable, dependable, reliable, able to detect error and heresy, and see the specious things that pass as gospel.

D. MARTYN LLOYD-JONES

UNBELIEF

Unbelief is not one of the grosser affections, but is that chief affection, seated and ruling on the throne of the will and reason . . . contrary to faith.

MARTIN LUTHER

We distinguish between the true and the spurious children, by the respective marks of faith and unbelief.

Nowadays unbelief overflows the whole earth, like a water flood.

Unbelief is the fountain of all evils.

As faith alone makes us obedient servants of God, and gives us up to His power, so unbelief makes us rebels and deserters.

Some portion of unbelief is always mixed with faith in every Christian.

Our own unbelief is no small hindrance to God's liberality.

It is a sure sign of unbelief not to be contented with the things that God gives us.

Our unbelief hinders God from displaying His power amongst us.

Most men nowadays either despise the gospel, or else are so infatuated that they dispute about it as though it were a trifle, or else simply make a mockery of it.

Nothing tends, more than distrust, to make us sluggish and useless.

JOHN CALVIN

I am made of unbelief, and cannot swim but where my feet may touch the ground.

SAMUEL RUTHERFORD

Melancholy [is] a great friend of unbelief.

Unbelief – this master-devil.

THOMAS BOSTON

Infidelity is, in general, a disease of the heart more than of the understanding.

WILLIAM WILBERFORCE

The Geneva pulpits (in 1817) violently opposed the doctrine of the Godhead of the Saviour, of original sin, of grace and effectual calling, and of predestination.

ROBERT HALDANE

UNBELIEF

(CONTINUED)

Not to have faith in God . . . is the highest offence which a creature can commit against its Creator . . . This sin is common and therefore is commonly disregarded.

Everywhere [in Scripture] atheism is regarded as a crime. Scripture always speaks of unbelief as a sin against God, and the special ground of the condemnation of the world (*John* 3:18).

CHARLES HODGE

Unbelief cannot speak . . . Faith loosens the tongue.

ALFRED EDERSHEIM

UNION WITH CHRIST

Faith in Christ is Christ Himself in thy heart.

AUGUSTINE

We are linked to our Lord Jesus Christ that He might dedicate us to His Father.

We are already set in the heavenly places, namely in the Person of our Head, Jesus Christ, who has knit and united us to Himself, never to be separated.

[Union with Christ] surpasses in greatness all the privileges our heart could conceive or imagine.

To 'sleep in Christ' (*1 Thess.* 4:13, 14) means to retain in death the union which we have with Christ.

[*On 1 Cor. 6:16*] The spiritual connection which we have with Christ belongs not merely to the soul, but also to the body (*Eph.* 5:30).

He who has Christ dwelling in him can want nothing.

In both dying and suffering we must be Jesus Christ's companions.

We are in Christ because we are out of ourselves. The mystical union, subsisting between Christ and His members should be matter of reflection, not only when we sit at the Lord's Table, but at all other times.

There is so great a unity between Christ and His members that the name of Christ sometimes includes the whole body, as in *1 Cor.* 12:12.

JOHN CALVIN

In this world believers are united to God by faith . . . In heaven it shall be by love.

There is . . . a nearer relation . . . between Christ and the Church, than ever was or can be between any other persons . . . A mystical [relation] such as between the head of a body and its members, or between a husband and his wife.

JOHN OWEN

[This union] is bestowed upon believers in their very first entrance into a holy state.

By union with Christ we partake of that spiritual life that He took possession of for us at His resurrection.

WALTER MARSHALL

The secret of holy living depends upon this doctrine of the union of the believer with Christ.

The effects of union with Christ are: 1. An interest in the merits of Christ, in order to our justification. 2. And the indwelling of His Spirit in order to our sanctification.

CHARLES HODGE

The Lord's Supper [is] the sacrament of union to and the sacrament of communion with Christ.

JAMES BANNERMAN

Every view of regeneration which does not do full justice to the 'mystical union with Christ' is anti-Scriptural, eradicates brotherly love, and begets spiritual pride.

ABRAHAM KUYPER

UNITY

By means of our Lord Jesus Christ we are so united together that there is a brotherhood between us which cannot be broken without forsaking the adoption which God has made of us.

JOHN CALVIN

Men that differ about bishops, ceremonies, and forms of prayer, may be all true Christians, and dear to one another and to Christ, if they be practically agreed in the life of godliness, and join in a holy,

heavenly conversation. But if you agree in all your opinions and formalities, and yet were never sanctified through the truth, you do but agree to delude your own souls, and none of you will be saved for all your agreement.

RICHARD BAXTER

It is not the actual differences of Christian men that are the mischief; but the mismanagement of those differences.

PHILIP HENRY

Notwithstanding all the sad divisions in our churches, the saints among us, so far as they are sanctified, are already one. The things in which they are agreed are . . .far more considerable, than are the things wherein they differ. They are of one mind concerning sin, that it is the worst thing in the world; concerning the favour of God, that it is better than life; concerning the world, that it is vanity; and concerning the Word of God, that it is above rubies.

MATTHEW HENRY

WISDOM

The conditions of wisdom are not so much intellectual as moral.

AUGUSTINE

Our wisdom ought to consist in embracing with gentle docility, without any exception, all that is delivered in the sacred Scriptures.

JOHN CALVIN

WISDOM

(CONTINUED)

It is the peculiar virtue of faith that we should willingly be fools, in order that we may learn to be wise only from the mouth of God.

Faith ought to be accompanied by prudence, that it may distinguish between the Word of God and the word of man.

He will so imprint His law in our hearts as we shall have a will agreeable to His, and then He shall overcome all temptations and accomplish that which He commands us.

It is our whole wisdom to inquire of His will.

God's wisdom is understood only by humility.

Our true wisdom is to overmaster ourselves.

The first step of wisdom is to ascribe nothing to ourselves.

This is all our wisdom, to take in good part whatsoever God appoints and does, and never ask why.

A man speaks with more or less wisdom, according as he has made more or less progress in the knowledge of Scripture.

In the Church all human traditions ought to be treated as worthless, since all men's wisdom is vanity and lies.

Athens . . . the mansion–house of wisdom, the fountain of all arts, the mother of humanity, exceeded all others in blindness and madness.

Spiritual wisdom . . . consists chiefly in three things — to know God; His paternal favour towards us, on which depends our salvation; and the method of regulating our lives according to the rule of the law.

All the gifts and power that men seem to possess are in the hand of God, so that He can, at any instant, deprive them of the wisdom which He has given them.

God will have none to be counted wise but Himself . . . All our wisdom must consist in hearkening unto Him.

The 'wisdom of the world', in Paul's acceptation, is that which assumes to itself authority, and does not allow itself to be regulated by the Word of God. Cursed be the wisdom which busies itself about the curious searching out of the . . . lower causes . . . and despises the Maker.

To search for wisdom, apart from Christ, means not simply foolhardiness, but utter insanity.

There is a heavenly and secret wisdom that is contained in the gospel, which cannot be apprehended by any acuteness or perspicacity of intellect . . . but by the revelation of the Spirit.

JOHN CALVIN

WORK

No labour is grievous to those who love it.

AUGUSTINE

Let us consider that God's registers are full of our works, words, and thoughts.

JOHN CALVIN

A leading secret of peace is work.

HENRY LIDDON

WORLD MISSION

[*In Matthew 28:19*] no certain limits are prescribed, but the whole world is assigned to [the apostles], to be reduced to obedience to Christ; that by disseminating the gospel wherever they could, they might erect His kingdom in all nations.

Christ was about to drive His plough through every country in the world.

It ought to be the object of our daily wishes that God would collect churches to Himself from all the countries of the earth, that He would enlarge their numbers, enrich them with gifts, and establish a legitimate order among them.

Even in our own time God so enriches certain churches more than others, that they may be seminaries to spread abroad the doctrine of the gospel.

May we daily solicit Thee in our prayers, and never doubt, but that under the government of Thy Christ, Thou canst again gather together the whole world.

JOHN CALVIN

John Calvin's Geneva was a school of missions. In 1561, the peak year, no less than 142 men ventured forth in their respective missions.

PHILIP E. HUGHES

Pray for the propagation of the gospel and kingdom of Jesus Christ to all nations; for the conversion of the Jews, the fullness of the Gentiles, the fall of Antichrist, and the hastening of the second coming of our Lord.

WESTMINSTER DIRECTORY FOR
PUBLIC WORSHIP

WORSHIP

The principle of worshipping God is a diligent love of Him.

The main thing in the worship of God is to embrace His promises with obedience.

We ought to bring nothing of our own when we worship God, but we ought to depend always on the Word of His mouth.

JOHN CALVIN

WORSHIP
(CONTINUED)

The rule for the worship of God ought to be taken from nothing else than from His own appointment.

Musical instruments in celebrating the praise of God would be no more suitable than the burning of incense, the lighting of lamps, and the restoration of the other shadows of the law.

One of the greatest benefits God can bestow upon us in this transitory life is to let us have some little corner wherein to assemble ourselves in His house.

God cannot be rightly worshipped unless when He has His peculiar attributes acknowledged.

Scripture frequently described the whole of worship as 'calling upon God'.

The chief object of life is to observe and worship God.

God is not properly worshipped but by the certainty of faith, which cannot be produced in any other way than by the Word of God.

God rejects, condemns, abominates all fictitious worship, and employs His Word as a bridle to keep us in unqualified obedience.

[On Psalm 138:1] The solemn assembly is, so to speak, a heavenly theatre graced by the presence of attending angels.

JOHN CALVIN

Adoration is the prostration of the soul before Christ as God.

JOHN OWEN

The duty of social worship lies in the law of nature itself . . . and is more especially necessitated by man's Fall.

JAMES BANNERMAN

The only holy place which we have is the heavenly sanctuary.

ADOLPH SAPHIR

Worship [is] adoration in act.

God has not willed to be adored without being obeyed.

ALEXANDRE VINET

[Believers] will receive nothing, practise nothing, own nothing in His worship but what is of His appointment.

W. H. GOOLD

A minister may have some excuse for despising a crowd, but never for despising two or three gathered together for worship.

G. D. HENDERSON

WORSHIP – CORRUPTED

We perceive in the human mind an intemperate longing for perverse worship.

God cannot dwell in a profane place. Nothing sanctifies a place more than obedience and sincerity of faith. When men introduce their inventions it immediately causes God to depart.

When we will invent services for God, according to our own fantasy, the pride is great.

Nothing is more easy than to corrupt the pure worship of God, when men esteem God after their sense and wit.

All self-invented services betray an impious contempt of God . . . The worship of God must be spiritual, in order that it may correspond with His nature.

All who seek instruction from statues or pictures gain nothing, but become entangled in the snares of Satan and find nothing but impostures . . . Who, by the sight of a picture or a statue can form a right idea of the true God? Is not the truth respecting Him thus turned to falsehood? . . . Is not His glory thus debased?

There is nothing to which men are more prone than to fall away from the pure worship of God.

The Papists place the spiritual worship of God in man's inventions.

[*On Joshua 22*] They sinned not lightly in attempting a novelty . . . and in a form which was very liable to be misconstrued . . . Let us learn to attempt nothing rashly . . . Let us beware of disturbing pious minds by the introduction of any kind of novelty.

Some inculcate acts of worship which are wicked and diametrically opposed to the Word of God. Others mingle profane trifles . . . adding to the Word of God some patches of their own inventions.

JOHN CALVIN

ZEAL

They who are the ensign bearers and are to govern the rest of the flock, must have a special liveliness in them above all others.

Where modesty is not, there the zeal is rash and not governed by the Spirit of God.

JOHN CALVIN

I could bear to be torn in pieces, if I could but hear the sobs of penitence, – if I could but see the eyes of faith directed to the Redeemer.

HENRY MARTYN

A zealous man in religion . . . burns for one thing; and that one thing is to please God, and to advance God's glory. If he is consumed in burning, he cares not for it– he is content.

J. C. RYLE

AUTHORS AND SOURCES

Alexander, Archibald (1772–1851), *Thoughts on Religious Experience,* 1844; reprinted London: Banner of Truth, 1967.

Alexander, W. L. (Bp.) (1808–44), *The Witness of the Psalms to Christ and Christianity*, John Murray, London 1877.

Alleine, Joseph (1634–68), *Memorial of Black Bartholomew,* 1662.

Anselm of Canterbury (1033–1109), churchman and theologian, author of *Cur Deus Homo*.

Augustine of Hippo (354–430), *Earlier Writings,* edited by J. H. S. Burleigh, London: SCM, 1953; and *Works*, edited by Marcus Dods, Edinburgh: T & T Clark, 1873.

Bacon, Francis, Lord (1561–1626), *Advancement of Learning & Novum Organum,* edited by J. Devey, London: Bell & Sons, 1876.

Baker's Dictionary of Theology, Grand Rapids: Baker Book House, 1966.

Bannerman, James (1807–68), *The Church of Christ*, 2 vols., 1869; reprinted London: Banner of Truth, 1960

Baxter, Richard (1615–91), *The Reformed Pastor*, 1656; reprinted Edinburgh, Banner of Truth, 1974.

Bede, the Venerable (673–735), churchman and historian, author of *History of the English Church and People*, Harmondsworth: Penguin, 1968.

Bengel, J. A. (1687–1752), Lutheran theologian, author of *Gnomon of the New Testament,* many editions.

Bethge, E., *Biography of Dietrich Bonhoeffer* (1906–45), Collins, 1970.

Bettensen, Henry, *The Early Christian Fathers (Clement to Athanasius)*, London: OUP, 1976.

Boettner, Loraine (1901–90), *The Reformed Doctrine of Predestination,* Grand Rapids: Eerdmans 1936.

Bonar, Andrew A. (1810–92), *Diary and Life,* edited by Marjory Bonar, 1893; reprinted London: Banner of Truth, 1960.

Bonar, Horatius (1808–89), *Memories of Dr Bonar,* Edinburgh: Oliphant, Anderson & Ferrier, 1909

Booth, General William (1829–1912), Salvation Army founder, quoted in W. A. Curtis, *History of Creeds and Confessions of Faith,* Edinburgh: T & T Clark, 1911.

Boston, Thomas (1676–1732), *Human Nature in Its Fourfold State,* London: Banner of Truth, 1960; *The Crook in the Lot,* 1861; *The Beauties of Boston,* 1831.

Bradford, John (1510–55), *Writings,* 2 vols., 1848; reprinted Edinburgh, Banner of Truth, 1979.

Bromiley, G. W., *Zwingli and Bullinger* in Library of Christian Classics, London: SCM, 1953.

Brown, David, *Life of the Late John Duncan* (1796–1870), 1872; reprinted Glasgow: Free Presbyterian Publications, 1986.

Brown, John (1722–87), quoted in Mackenzie, Robert, *John Brown of Haddington,* London: Banner of Truth, 1964.

Brunner, Emil (1889–1966), *Man in Revolt,* Lutterworth, 1939; and *The Divine Imperative,* quoted in Baker's Dictionary of Theology, 1960.

Buchanan, James (1804–70) *The Doctrine of Justification,* 1867; reprinted London: Banner of Truth, 1961.

Bunyan, John (1628–88), *The Holy War; The Pilgrim's Progress; Grace Abounding to the Chief of Sinners* (many editions).

Cairns, John (1818–92), *Unbelief in the Eighteenth Century,* Edinburgh: T & T Clark, 1880.

Calvin, John (1509–64), *Commentaries on the Old and New Testaments*, Edinburgh: Calvin Translation Society; *Institutes of the Christian Religion* (many editions); *Sermons on Ephesians*, Edinburgh: Banner of Truth, 1973; *Sermons on Timothy & Titus,* Banner of Truth, 1983; *Sermons on 2 Samuel: 1–13*, Banner of Truth, 1992; *Sermons on Deuteronomy*, Banner of Truth, 1987; *Sermons on Job*, Banner of Truth, 1993; *Sermons on Galatians*, Banner of Truth, 1997; *Selected Letters*, Banner of Truth, 1980; *Tracts*, 3 vols., Calvin Translation Society, 1849.

Candlish, J. S. (1835–97), *The Kingdom of God*, Edinburgh: T & T Clark, 1884.

Candlish, Robert S. (1806–73), *Life in a Risen Saviour*, Edinburgh: A & C Black, 1859.

Carmichael, Amy Wilson (1868–1951), missionary to India. Her writings include *Rose from Briar* (1950) and *Gold Cord* (1952).

Carrell, Alexis (1873–1944), scientist, author of *Man the Unknown*, Pelican, 1948.

Chalmers, Thomas (1780–1847), quoted in James Buchanan, *The Doctrine of Justification* (see above).

Chambers, Oswald (1874–1917), *Memoir by His Widow*, London: Simpkin, Marshall, 1933.

Charnock, Stephen (1628–80), Puritan minister and author.

Chrysostom, John (c. 347–407), preacher and Greek Church father.

Cowper, William (1731–1800), poet, hymnwriter and associate of John Newton; *Olney Hymns*, Edinburgh: James Taylor, no date; *Poetical Works*, Glasgow, Dunn and Wright, no date.

Cragg, G. R., *The Church and the Age of Reason*, Pelican, 1960.
Cromwell, Oliver (1599–1658), *Letters and Speeches*, edited by Thomas Carlyle, London: Chapman and Hall, 1893.

Cullman, Oscar (b. 1902) *Christ and Time*, London: SCM, 1951.

Cumming, J. Elder (1807–81), *Through the Eternal Spirit*, Stirling: Drummond Tract Depot, no date.

Cunningham, William (1805–61), *The Reformers and the Theology of the Reformation*, 1862; reprinted London: Banner of Truth, 1969.

Durham, James (1622–58), Scottish minister and author of *Clavis Cantici* (on the Song of Solomon), reprinted, Aberdeen, 1840.

Edersheim, Alfred (1825–89), *The Life and Times of Jesus the Messiah*, 2 vols., London: Longmans, Green & Co, 1887.

Edwards, Jonathan (1703–58), *Treatise on the Religious Affections*, 1746; reprinted London: Banner of Truth, 1961; *Charity and its Fruits*, 1852; reprinted Banner of Truth, 1969

Eusebius (c. 265–c. 339), churchman and theologian.

Flavel, John (1628–91), Puritan minister and writer.

Flint, Robert (1838–1910). Quoted in Macmillan, Donald, *The Life of Dr Robert Flint,* Edinburgh: Hodder & Stoughton, 1914.

Fuller, Thomas (1608–61), *The Holy and Profane States*, 1642.

Girdlestone, Canon R. B., author of *Synonyms of the Old Testament*, 1897; reprinted Grand Rapids: Eerdmans, 1976.

Goold, Rev. W. H. (1815–97), editor of the *Works of John Owen*, 1850–3; reprinted London: Banner of Truth, 1965–8.

Graham, Billy, quoted in John Pollock's *Biography*, 1966.

Guinness, Henry Grattan (1835–1910), preacher and writer.

Haldane, James (1768–1851) and Robert (1764–1842), described in Alexander Haldane, *The Lives of the Haldanes*, 1852; reprinted Edinburgh: Banner of Truth, 1990.

Hallesby, Ole Kristian (1879–1961), Norwegian theologian, author of *Conscience*, London: Hodder & Stoughton, 1939, and *Prayer* (many editions).

Henderson, G. D., *The Claims of the Church of Scotland*, 1951.

Hengstenberg, Ernst (1802–69), German theologian.

Henry, Philip (1631–96), Puritan minister, father of Matthew Henry (1662–1714), the Bible commentator.

Hodge, Charles (1797–1878), author of *Systematic Theology, The Church and its Polity, The Way of Life* and many commentaries.

Howe, John (1630–1705), Puritan minister and author of *The Living Temple of God*, quoted in John Smeaton's *The Doctrine of The Holy Spirit*.

Hughes, Philip E., editor, *The Register of the Company of Pastors in Geneva in the Time of Calvin*, Grand Rapids: Eerdmans, 1966.

Ignatius (c. 40–117), theologian and bishop of Antioch. See *Early Christian Fathers*, Library of Christian Classics, London: SCM, 1953.

Irenaeus (c. 130–200), theologian and bishop of Lyons. Cited in Bettensen, *Early Christian Fathers*, 1956.

Jeffreys, Prof. M. C. V., educationist, author of *Glaucon, An Inquiry into the Aims of Education*, Pitman, 1950.

Jerome (c. 345–419), theologian and biblical critic.

Justin Martyr (c. 155), early Christian apologist.

Kelly, J. N. D., *Early Christian Creeds*, London: Longmans, 1967.

Kirn, O., theologian, quoted by B. B. Warfield in *The Person and Work of Christ* (Presbyterian and Reformed, 1930).

Knox, John (1514–72), Scottish Reformer, his *History of the Reformation in Scotland* has been republished by the Banner of Truth, 1982.

Kuyper, Abraham (1837–1920), *The Work of the Holy Spirit*, New York: Funk & Wagnalls, 1900.

Latimer, Hugh (1485–1555), Reformer and martyr. *Sermons and Remains*, Cambridge: Parker Society, 1845.

Lecerf, Auguste (1872–1943), French Reformed theologian and author of *Introduction to Reformed Dogmatics*, London, 1949.

Leighton, Robert (1611–84), author of a noted commentary on 1 Peter. See E. A. Knox, *Robert Leighton, Archbishop of Glasgow*, London: J. Clarke & Co, 1930.

Lenski, R. C. H., Lutheran Bible commentator.

Liddon, Henry P. (1829–90), *Easter in St Paul's*, London: Longmans, Green & Co, 1897; *The Divinity of Our Lord*, Bampton Lectures, 1866.

Livingstone, John (1603–72), Scottish Covenanting minister.

Lloyd-Jones, D. M. (1899–1981), *Preaching and Preachers*, London: Hodder & Stoughton, 1971

Luthardt, C. E. (1823–1902), *The Saving Truths of Christianity; The Moral Truths of Christianity*, Edinburgh: T & T Clark, 1872 and 1889.

Luther, Martin (1483–1546), *Selected Works*, edited by Dillenberger, New York: Anchor Books, 1961; *First Lectures on the Psalms*, 2 vols., St Louis: Concordia, 1974; *The Bondage of the Will* (many editions).

Machen, J. Gresham (1881–1937), *God Transcendent*, Edinburgh: Banner of Truth, 1982.

MacPhail, Simeon R., *Bible Class Handbook on Colossians*, Edinburgh: T & T Clark, 1911.

Melville, Andrew (1545–1622), quoted in McCrie, C. G., *Life of Andrew Melville*.

Marshall, Walter (1628–80), *The Gospel Mystery of Sanctification*, Edinburgh: J. Taylor, 1973.

Martin, Hugh (1822–85), *The Atonement*, Edinburgh: Knox Press, 1976.

Martyn, Henry (1780–1812), quoted in H. C. G. Moule, *Life of Charles Simeon*, London: Methuen, 1905.

M'Cheyne, Robert Murray (1813–43), eminent Scottish minister.

Miller, Rev. Thomas of New Zealand, see *Introduction*.

Morris, Leon (b. 1914), quoted in *Baker's Dictionary of Theology*.

Moody, D. L. ((1837–99), quoted in W. R. Moody, *Life of D. L. Moody*, Kilmarnock: John Ritchie, no date.

Murray, John (1898–1975), *Redemption Accomplished and Applied*, London: Banner of Truth, 1961; *Collected Writings*, 4 vols., Banner of Truth, 1982.

Nazianzen, Gregory (c. 329–89), Cappadocian father.

Newman, J. H. (1801–90), *The Idea of a University*, London, 1873

Niesel, W. (1903–88), *Reformed Dogmatics*, Edinburgh: Oliver & Boyd, 1962.

Nisbet, John (d. 1685), Scottish Covenanting martyr.

O'Brien, J. T. (Bp.), *The Nature and Effects of Faith*, London: Macmillan, 1863.

Orr, James (1844–1913), *Sidelights on Christian Doctrine*, London: Marshall Bros, 1909.

Owen, John (1616–83), *Works*, 1850–3; reprinted, London: Banner of Truth, 1965–8.

Pascal, Blaise (1623–62), *Thoughts on Religion and Philosophy*, London: Kegan Paul, 1889.

Pearson, John (Bp.) (1613–86), *Exposition of the Creed*, London, 1866.

Reid, W. Stanford (1913–96), *Trumpeter of God*, A Life of John Knox, New York, Scribners, 1974.

Rutherford, Samuel (1600–61), *Letters*, edited by Andrew Bonar, Edinburgh: Oliphant, Anderson & Ferrier, 1891.

Ryle, J. C. (1816–1900), *Christian Leaders of the Eighteenth Century*, 1885; reprinted Edinburgh: Banner of Truth, 1978.

Saphir, Adolph (1831–91), *Christ and the Scriptures*, London: Morgan & Scott, no date; *The Divine Unity of Scripture*, London: Hodder & Stoughton, 1894.

Schaff, Philip (1819–93), *The Person of Christ*, Doran, 1913.

Shedd, W. G. T. (1820–94), *Homiletics and Pastoral Theology*, Edinburgh: Oliphants, 1869.

Simeon, Charles (1759–1836), quoted in H. C. G. Moule, *Life of Charles Simeon*, London: Methuen, 1905.

Smeaton, George (1814–89), *Our Lord's Doctrine of the Atonement; The Apostles' Doctrine of the Atonement*, 1870; reprinted Edinburgh: Banner of Truth, 1991.

Smellie, Alexander, *The Men of the Covenant*, 1903; reprinted London: Banner of Truth, 1960.

Spurgeon, C. H. (1834–92), *An All Round Ministry*, 1900; reprinted London: Banner of Truth, 1960.

Stuart, A. Moody (1808–98), quoted in biography by K. Moody Stuart, London: Hodder & Stoughton, 1899.

Swete, H. B. (1835–1917), *The Holy Catholic Church*, London: Macmillan, 1913.

Tasker, R. V. G., *The Old Testament in the New Testament*, Grand Rapids: Eerdmans, 1954.

Taylor, W. M., author of *The Scottish Pulpit from the Reformation to the Present Day*.

Tertullian (c. 155–220), first Latin church father.

Thornwell, J. H. (1812–62), *Life and Letters*, 1875, reprinted Edinburgh: Banner of Truth, 1974.

Tregelles, S. P. (1813–75), *Introduction to Gesenius' Hebrew and Chaldee Lexicon*, London: Bagsters, 1885.

Trevelyan, G. M., *History of England*, 1926.

Tyndale, William (c. 1494–1536), *The Obedience of a Christian Man* (1528).

Vinet, Alexander (1797–1847), *Outlines of Theology*, London: Strahan, 1866; *Pastoral Theology*, Edinburgh: T & T Clark, 1855.

Warfield, Benjamin B. (1851–1921), *The Person and Work of Christ*, Presbyterian & Reformed, 1930; *Perfectionism*, 2 vols, OUP, 1931; *Calvin and Augustine*, Presbyterian & Reformed, 1956.

Wesley, John (1703–91), *Journal*, edited by N. Curnock, London: Epworth, 1958.

Westcott, B. F. (1825–1901), *The Gospel of the Resurrection*, London: Macmillan, 1867.

Whitefield, George (1714–70), *Journals*, 1738–41; partially reprinted London: Banner of Truth, 1965; see also biography by Arnold Dallimore, 2 vols., Banner of Truth, 1970; 1980.

Whyte, Alexander (1836–1921), Scottish preacher and writer.

Wilberforce, William (1759–1833), *The Prevailing Religious System of Professed Christians in the Higher Middle Classes in This Country, Contrasted with Real Christianity*, London: Longman Green, 1865.

Zwingli, Ulrich (1484–1531), quoted in *Zwingli and Bullinger*, edited by G. W. Bromiley, London: SCM, 1950.